Nickie's Nook

Sharing the Journey

Nickie Coby

Copyright 2007

www.nickiesnook.com

ISBN 978-0-6151-5423-7

Nickie's Nook

Copyright and Publisher Information

Text Copyright 2007 by Nickie Coby

http://www.nickiesnook.com

Cover Art Copyright 2007

Helena Coby

Further examples of her work can be viewed at

http://flickr.com/photos/hmcoby/

ISBN 978-0-6151-5423-7

Author's Note

I encourage you to do whatever you need to more easily read this book. Scanning, exporting or otherwise changing the format of this book to make it more accessible and useful to you is acceptable. However, if you should pass on a file which you have created from this book, please include this copyright page and encourage the users of the file to purchase their own copy.

This book has been self-published on LuLu

http://www.lulu.com/

Dedication

This book is dedicated to anyone who suffers from chronic pain, and especially Complex Regional Pain Syndrome and those who walk beside us on this painful journey. You are not alone.

Also, to those wonderful instructors and raisers who nurture dogs to become guides. Thank you for my partner.

Table of Contents

Table of Contents	iv
A Beginning Word or More…	1
An Introduction to This Volume	3
Acknowledgements	7
Humor	9
One thing I won't buy…	9
I was drunk the day my Mama got out of Prison[1]: Or, my two alcohol-related experiences…	9
Nickie's Secret Diet!	10
…And I don't think squirrels flush…	11
Important Tip…	12
Today's lesson in resourcefulness: Opening a LidoDerm pack with a stylus…	12
Seeing red…	13
Sign #33 I'm 'White and Nerdy'…	14
In case Julio reads this blog…	14
Stories of Julio	15

Julio Blogs — 32

Clicker training — 37

Kid in a candy store — 37
Who's training who? — 38
A quick click — 38
Shape up... — 39

Writings I'm especially proud of — 42

CRPS: The Condition of Hell — 42

Works Cited — 69

Never Forsaken — 71

An Unseen and Unknown Hero: The Guide — 78

Brewberry's on a Sunday Morning — 82

A Work Of Art — 85

Ablism In Healthcare — 88

Missing Confidentiality — 89
Missing the Point — 92
Missing Access — 93

Keeping It to Ourselves	94
People First, Disabilities Later	96
A Little Creativity Goes a Long Way	97
The Method	97
Context	98

The New Empowered You — **100**

A New Lease on Access — **114**

Transitioning To College: Ways To Make Sure You Grow And Enjoy! — **118**

Know your resources: Build a tool box	118
Manage your stress and schedule	120
Asking for Help Makes You More Independent	121
Take It Slow	122
Putting it all together	123

Relaxation — **124**

Premise	124
Exercise #1: Prayer	124
Exercise #2: Blogging	125
Exercise #3: Breathe	125
Exercise #4: Imagery	125
Exercise #5: Relaxing your muscles	126
Exercise #6: Aesthetic Appreciation	126

> *Exercise #7: Listen to music*   127

Freedom from Fear and a Chance to Grow   129

Assisting a Guide Dog Team   134

> *Looking for a Good Route*   134
> *Seeking a good landmark*   135
> *Dos and Don'ts for Teaching the Team*   136
> *How the Team Crosses a Street*   137
> *A Few Definitions and Concepts*   138
> *Further Assistance*   140
> *Acknowledgements*   140

The Philosophy of Guide Dog Public Relations   141

The Intersection of Pain and Blindness   149

> *Biological and Physical*   151
> *Psychological*   160
> *Social*   166
> *Spiritual*   167

Independence? Interdependence?   170

He Leads Me: Reflections on Trust and Faith   174

Smile! You're on Crossing Camera!   177

Accessible social media: It's not just for fun anymore. 182

Shining light on hope: What Barabbas can teach us. 186

Peace and Hope 190

Election 2006: My own personal victory 193

So... What's my Tapestry? 197

A Beginning Word or More…

This book is born of my blog, Nickie's Nook, and some of the best entries I've written there. I want to first thank you for picking up this book. Whatever reasons caused you to read these words, I hope it exceeds your expectations.

I wrote this book because I hope that my journey can help others know they are not alone. I hope that my ideas can help you find peace and hope.

Who is Nickie? I'm a college student, attending a private college in the Midwest United States. I am blind, though I can see light and bright colors. I travel with a wonderful Guide Dog named Julio. I suffer from Complex Regional Pain Syndrome, a condition characterized by extreme burning pain. I am a social work major who hopes to work with people who suffer from pain. Finally, I am a Christian.

As you can see, there are many facets of my identity. You will notice this throughout this book, as I write about my life and multiple strands of who I am shine through.

I hope you enjoy reading.

Sincerely,
Nickie Coby

An Introduction to This Volume

With so many books being published each year, and the relative ease of self-publishing, why should you pick up this book? Like me, you've probably got a few books which you haven't read yet piled somewhere. I know that frustration, and I sympathize with the struggle. Every author thinks YOU should read THEIR book and recommend it to your friends. As the author of this book, I admit I have a vested interest in you enjoying the book and sharing it with friends. I want to prepare you to read this book, and encourage you to read it and think as you read. Below, I've included some explanations which I hope will help you understand this book better and make your reading experience more valuable.

What I've included in this book is mostly my own experience. However, I have tried to think deeper and wider about the topics I present. Many of the essays, stories, papers and articles here were designed to open the minds of others. I wanted to make sure that others would know what it is like living with a visible and a not-so-visible disability. My goal is to dispel misconceptions and false impressions of people with disabilities or chronic pain.

I noticed differences in the way I approach my pain and the way I approach blindness. Moreover, I could find very few sources of accessible information that applied to someone trying to work through chronic pain in addition to blindness. So many times, I found myself in situations where what I should do as a person with pain and what I should do as a blind person were almost completely opposite from each other.

Writing a book has always been a dream for me. As soon as I realized I enjoyed writing, I dreamed of writing a book, maybe a novel, even. The problem is that I dislike having someone edit, proofread or otherwise criticize my work. I also realized that books can reach where blogs do not. A book can go anywhere, even when you don't have a computer. Books can be given as gifts. And books are sometimes easier to navigate when you aren't sure where to start.

What I have attempted to create is a book you can turn to for reassurance, inspiration and ideas. I've shared some of what works for me, and some of what doesn't. Use this book as a stepping stone for your own blog, journal or other form of writing and contemplation.

You can use this book to remind you that you are not alone in your struggles. It can be a source of encouragement and assistance as you approach your own life. Some of what I do may work for you, and some of it may not. If you find yourself thinking *How come x doesn't work for me,* while reading typical sources of information on a disability or chronic illness, you might enjoy knowing that it's okay, desirable even, to not fit into the box so many people love to put us in.

Finally, use this book to challenge your own thinking. Read about some of what I've learned. Maybe you are in the medical field and feel uncomfortable around people with chronic pain or people who are blind. Maybe you believe chronic pain doesn't exist or that young people never get it. Maybe you think that blind people are amazing just for getting out of bed and finding the bathroom. Whatever thoughts you have, please consider leaving them at home as you walk through my written journey. If you're reading this in your home, simply ignore your previous notions if they get in the way of your reading. If they are helpful to you, by all means, use them as you read! I don't want you to agree with me, all I ask is that you consider learning from my experiences.

Advocacy comes in many forms; for me, this book

is a form of advocacy. How can people accommodate needs if they don't know what those needs are? Please learn about us; we're not so different in what we want, we just have to get at it in different ways. I use a Guide Dog, Julio, and a support cane to walk, for example. Someone who is blind can still enjoy reading, but we'll use Braille or audio books to do it. I write in print or Braille, and enjoy it just as others do. My desires are similar to yours, I desire a full life. I may have different challenges, but my needs are as valid as yours. Know that my needs aren't always the same as people who are blind or others with chronic pain, but getting to know me may help your comfort level.

Each piece I've written has something to share. I hope they give you much to consider.

Finally, if I can answer any questions, please don't hesitate to contact me (my contact information is in the title page of this book.)

Acknowledgements

Many people have knowingly and unknowingly contributed to the process of creating this book. I first wish to thank my parents, who believed that their daughter should have the same opportunities as any sighted child. My sister Helena, who puts up with all of the questions I would never ask my parents. Marlaina, who has encouraged me, cried with me, challenged me and loved me. You gave me the courage to try.

I also wish to thank many other friends who have shared their lives with me, and never held anything back. Your friendships have provided strength that can only come from sharing life with others. Dee, Jeff, Jen, Michael and Anessa have walked through my journey, pushing me to think hard, work hard, pray, play and laugh hard. Without your love and support, I would not be writing this.

All of the readers of Nickie's Nook who wrote comments and emails, sharing their stories and offering support made me believe that my writing was worth reading. Without you, I wouldn't believe a book was possible.

To the instructors who taught Julio to guide and taught me to follow, you gave me a gift no one else could. To the wonderful family who raised Julio and loved him enough to let him go, you gave me the confidence I need to walk into new situations. This has transferred to my writing.

Humor

One thing I won't buy...

So we were looking up pizza places online. The only advertised link said "'Za: Whatever you're looking for, you can find it on eBay." I'm sorry, but if it's used, I refuse to bid.

I was drunk the day my Mama got out of Prison[1]: Or, my two alcohol-related experiences...

I told you I was having a creative slump, and a friend made a post that reminded me of these experiences. So, I thought I'd write them down in lieu of an entry that's productive, not sure if they have been written in this space before.

Eighth grade: I accidentally brought a beer to school. We'd had people over that weekend, and, trying to be helpful, they'd turned the beers right side up (we

---

[1] Adapted from "You Never Even Called Me By My Name" by S. Goodman, recorded by David Allen Coe

always kept them upside down just for this reason). It was my job to grab my drink for my lunch bag; that morning I did so. Mom didn't look at it (we never had this problem before). At lunch, I opened the can and let's just say it did NOT smell like soda. I shoved it in the bag and ran (don't do that with a cane) to the trash can. One of the guidance counselors asked if I was okay. "Just fine," I said.

    Late ninth grade: I'm in a singing group and we're singing at a church. It's communion Sunday, so we all go up. First we get these wafers, which stick to my mouth. I figure I'll just get it down with the grape juice. I've never made such a face in my life!

Nickie's Secret Diet!
    Since I can't exactly get a job right now, I'm thinking of ways to earn some money. Here's what I've come up with. After all, if I can't turn the surgery into something positive, I can at least try to make money off of it right?

    So, here's what I plan to do. Everyone's reading diet books. I could become a fitness coach. All I ask of my participants is the following:

    1. Have a surgery, and a reaction to anesthetic.
    2. Get sick, don't eat for a day.

3. Purchase a walker and hop around to get places for eight weeks.

4. Get nauseated from pain killers.

I know it works. I haven't been weighed yet, but I may have lost up to an inch and a half around my lumbar area. How do I know this? When I was in school, before the surgery, and needed a block, they used a six inch long needle. Two weeks ago, they used a four and a half inch one. Go figure! And, in case you were unsure, no, I won't write a diet book.

...And I don't think squirrels flush...

I'm going to attempt to capture a stream of consciousness on paper, after it actually happened. I don't usually write stream of consciousness, so please be patient with me.

Hmm... I wonder what the bloggers are writing about today. Listening... Click "add to del.icio.us". Click. Nah.

Where's Baxter going? Is there a squirrel in the house? I hope Baxter doesn't try to kill it. Hmm... That sounds like a big squirrel. Click, click post.

That's a really big squirrel. Wait, I don't think squirrels can shut doors, can they? And I don't know of any squirrels that can flush. Is someone in the house?

Should I call 911? Should I call Dad at work? No, he can't do anything. (This is when I start praying really, really hard.)

I think someone's in the house. They're coming this way. "Who is that???!"

Turns out it was dad all along! And I still don't think squirrels can flush toilets.

Important Tip…

If you're going to write a relaxation tape, don't use the image of a person's nostrils as exhaust pipes, no matter how perfect you think the image is.

Today's lesson in resourcefulness: Opening a LidoDerm pack with a stylus…

Who says using a slate and stylus for Braille can't pay off in more than one area of your life? Did you know your stylus can help you open packages? It's a great tool when your scissors seem to have walked off and you need your LidoDerm, for example. Here's how to open a LidoDerm pack with a stylus:

1. Find the corner of the LidoDerm pack, away from the patch.

2. Carefully hold the pack so that your fingers are out of the way of where you'll be working, but so that they provide stability to the corner.

3. Place stylus in the corner, about a quarter inch in, or just far enough to avoid the reinforced side of the package.

4. Press down with the stylus until a hole is formed.

5. Pull the stylus toward the side of the package, forming a slit.

6. Use the slit as leverage to open the package.

7. Ask a friend to help you find your scissors when it's not after quiet hours.

Seeing red...

For once, it's not that I'm seeing red because my eye is demonstrating why I don't rely on my vision for tasks (as if seeing me with Julio wouldn't prove that or something). This is the part where I tell an embarrassing story about myself.

We went to dinner this evening, since my grandma is here for the holidays. I'd ordered a cherry Coke, and didn't realize it was in front of me. Dad mentioned it, and I was looking for it. Well, I found it, as it went flying. Julio got drenched. He looked up like

"WTF?" (I don't use that much, but it fits well here). Then, when he figured it out, he looked like he was the happiest puppy in the world, and started drinking. It was like he was thinking "It's manna from heaven. Praise the Lord and Hallelujah!!!!"

It looked a bit like I had Clifford for a guide dog. I can just see the people at the table next to us going home and saying "So this blind chick spilled all over her dog..." Very embarrassing... At least it makes an interesting post though.

Sign #33 I'm 'White and Nerdy'...
Weather web site: "A broad band of snow..."
Me: "OOH, broadband?"

In case Julio reads this blog...
Dear Julio
I know that you are a talented Labrador, but really, it isn't necessary to steal stuff off the tables when I leave to go to the bathroom. Paper towels and M&Ms offer nothing of value to your body. Moreover, these things are actually important to me. And, in case you didn't know, chocolate is really bad for you.
Love,
Mommy/Nickie/a ticked off young woman

Stories of Julio

At the end of my senior year, I briefly worked on a blog to share my experiences of high school with a guide dog. I wanted to give people an idea of Julio's and my life together. These are most of the entries from that blog.

Http://juliostories.blogspot.com/

Wednesday, April 27, 2005

Weirded-out Wednesday

The fun thing about graduating is that your family gets to spend money on paper that tells other people you're graduating. And that's not cool when you have a bad right arm and need to carry a box of grad announcements through the busy halls. Other than a few stolen morsels from the floor, Julio handled this better than I did! I think he's unhappy about the snow though.

Posted by Nickie at 5:43 PM

Thursday, April 28, 2005

A sticky situation

As I sat in first hour with that blank look of exhaustion on my face and my spearmint Eclipse in my mouth, I thought mostly about the book Staggerford.

Then, the unthinkable; my gum fell out of my mouth. I didn't find it... Until third hour when I couldn't get Julio's harness off. It was stuck on with the gum. My journalism instructor helped cut it out of his fur.

Posted by Nickie at 6:48 PM

Saturday, April 30, 2005

Retreat! Retreat!

Having a Guide Dog is fun, but it takes communication. Not only do you have to tell your dog where to go, but you have to talk to others.

I was on a retreat last night and at 9 PM, I was getting tired. Someone came up and started petting Julio while he was doing his business. Or at least, that's what he was supposed to be doing.

When I'm tired, I don't necessarily communicate with the nicest, kindest attitude. My first response is to tell people where to get off. "Can't you see he's trying to pee? How would you like to have to pee in a parking lot with someone trying to pet you? You want to stand out for a long time with him with no jacket?"

Luckily for the unsuspecting person, I just told them that I was trying to get my dog to go to the bathroom. I think they were surprised.

"Is that your Guide Dog?"

"Yeah,"

"Oh," (person starts petting the dog.)

"Julio, do your business!"

"What?"

"I'm trying to get him to go to the bathroom."

"Oh, I just want to pet him."

"Sorry, he needs to go. It's better if you don't pet Guide Dogs."

"Oh."

"Thanks for asking though."

This morning, in the elevator on the way down in the morning, Julio was distracted. Pop goes the leash correction.

"He's just saying hi!"

"He's not supposed to do that though."

"Oh, that's my fault."

I wanna put the collar on you and give you the correction!

That last part was a thought, not said out loud.

Just proof that I can't be my crabby self all the time.

Nickie's Nook

Posted by Nickie at 4:20 PM

Sunday, May 01, 2005
Walk proud

This morning I woke up and groaned. I didn't know what I was thinking doing the Walk America for March of Dimes thing with tendonitis in my foot. I got up, ate breakfast and headed for the school.

I ended up making a new friend before we even left the school. Three of us, including the driver, got into the car and another group drove as well.

When we got there, it was way, way cold. One of the girls let me borrow a glove for my left hand. We had bagels and coffee from Panera's. It was good, but I wasn't a fan of the coffee. It warmed us up though.

We went around the little stands of sponsors where there was free stuff. Then finally, the walk started. Throughout all this, I had to keep wraps on Julio since there were lots of dogs. It ended up being so fun though!

Julio did a great job! We ended up walking about 4.5 miles before my foot gave out.

Let me just say that without Julio, the walk wouldn't have been nearly as fun! It was so nice to keep up with the group without going sighted guide. Julio did great!

I did have to consider his needs, but that wasn't hard. He'll drink from a paper cup if necessary so I just gave him water that way. It was really amazing!

I was cold by the end, but actually, I stayed relatively warm while we were moving!

Definitely, this was one of the great experiences that having a dog made possible!

Posted by Nickie at 7:05 PM

Wednesday, May 04, 2005

Pop Goes the Weasel

Around and round the cafeteria, the Guide Dog chases the food.

The Guide Dog thinks it's all in fun...

Pop goes the leash correction.

Ah, the fun of food distractions. He is slowly getting better.

Posted by Nickie at 5:42 PM

The ultimate distraction and college campuses

Yesterday, I went on a mobility lesson to the college I'll be attending next year. It was a really productive visit since Julio and I were communicating well.

Julio handled the curves and twists of the campus well. I had some issues with time distance estimation. For anyone who's not familiar with this, with a cane, you find lots of landmarks. You feel the poles, bumps and cracks. A dog will guide around those things (usually), so you have to be aware of other things. Sometimes, you can use sounds or the slants of a sidewalk, but other times, you have to time yourself a little bit. I messed up, but together, we figured it out.

Julio and I learned where the dorm we'll possibly be staying in is. We even took a tour of it. It looks like an easy dorm to find. Julio and I really did well at finding things yesterday.

So on the way back, a squirrel crossed our path, but it wasn't just your run-of-the-mill squirrel. No, it was the kind that crossed directly in front of Julio... Not smart of that squirrel. But it was also carrying a graham cracker or something. Julio just looked and went on. Yes, I think we're starting to understand each other.

Posted by Nickie at 9:55 PM

Saturday, May 07, 2005
Public Relations
One of the unfortunate side effects of having a Guide Dog is dealing with the public. Please don't get

me wrong, this can be a huge positive. I love answering honest questions from people who are genuinely curious. What I don't enjoy is dealing with people who don't think appropriate behavior applies to them.

This can be as simple as not listening to my request, the sign Julio wears, other people or all three. My least favorite comment from people is "Come on you've gotta let me pet him." The truth is that I don't. I'm not the most assertive person in the world, but in this case, I have to be. It may sound selfish for me to refuse petting to someone, but it is actually very important to be firm. If you've ever seen how excited a dog gets to be petted, you know how hard it can be to get their attention back on you. It's not a matter of being mean; it's a matter of safety.

Next on the list is "I know I'm not supposed to but…" Usually, this is followed by the person reaching down and petting my dog. If you know you're not supposed to, why do you do it?

I also hate questions people ask just to make me angry. There's a difference between respectful questions and just asking for your own amusement.

If you're considering getting a Guide Dog, you should also be aware that there will be times when you won't eat a warm lunch/dinner/breakfast. For one, sometimes your dog will be distracted by food and you'll have to correct him or her. For two, you'll need to answer questions. Sometimes, this is a good thing. I've seen people really learn a lot and sometimes, it's really helpful for both of us. But sometimes, you'll find yourself caught in a conversation with no end in sight. You can be assertive, but you don't want to burn your bridges. What I mean is you don't want to give people a bad impression of Guide Dogs as a whole.

Oh and the fake comments about what your dog is doing are not cool. I've had people tell me my dog has bitten them. Other sighted people have confirmed that he didn't. Others will tell me my dog has eaten something he shouldn't. This is hard to deal with because you don't want to punish your dog if he didn't do anything. But if your dog did something, a correction is in order.

Sometimes, public interactions can be pleasant. You can find people who are willing to help you find a location. You can meet others who know someone who wants a guide. It's nice to have an automatic conversation starter. You just have to balance these things out.

Posted by Nickie at 8:15 PM

Sunday, May 08, 2005

Backfiring

I found these really cute little, little treats that I was giving to Baxter and Julio. Julio, of course, is my Guide Dog and Baxter is my pet dog. I gave Julio a treat and I almost gave Baxter a treat, but Julio took it. Just goes to show that you have to be careful when treating your dog, especially in front of others!

Posted by Nickie at 9:24 PM

My favorite quote of late

Just trying to be fair to Julio:

Dad, to Baxter: "I pet his ears and he smiles. I pet your ears and you chew on me!"

Guide Dogs are good, Baxters are... Um... Not sure what they are.

Posted by Nickie at 9:32 PM

Tuesday, May 10, 2005

You'll have a field day with this one!

Two of my classes are college in the schools classes. This means that they are college classes, but they are taught in the high school. The work is comparable to that of a college class; it's just a different location.

Today, the literature class I'm in had a field day at the university sponsoring the college in the schools program. With a cane, I usually felt disoriented in a new environment. Because I did not feel comfortable walking quickly with a cane, I often went sighted guide to save time. Today, with Julio, I did not need to do that! I was able to have people give me directions without worrying if I would poke someone in the heels, bump into something or any of the other things which frustrated me.

When we got to the university, I relieved Julio. This was really important since he drank quite a bit of water this morning.

My teacher walked with me and just told me when I needed to turn. Julio and I had our first experience (that I remember) with spiral staircases. Julio did well, although I think he was a little bit afraid.

We found a seat in the auditorium and Julio settled at my feet and didn't move for the entire lecture. I focused on taking notes and absorbing information about post-modernism.

When it was time to break up into small groups, we had to go to a separate building. Julio and I simply followed our group leader, who happened to be a teacher from our school. Again, I got directions and we made it to the classroom quickly. I focused on discussion and journaling. Then, we headed back to the auditorium where I even presented my story.

After this, my mobility instructor and I met up and we headed off for lunch. She gave me instructions and I was able to execute the route with very few complications. I did have to relieve Julio again. This also involved looking for a trash can.

I had been to this establishment a few times, so I was able to figure out where the entrance was. Once inside, I used a gentle leader on Julio so he'd behave around all the food. Lunch was good and Julio needed just a few reminders to settle down. We walked to the parking garage. Julio was distracted by people and a dog. I focused his attention with some obedience. Now at this point with a cane, I'd be shot. I'd want to go home and rest. But I still had energy, so we visited my college again.

I was able to practice a familiar route, pick up some medicine for a headache and some caffeine, find the restroom then leave the building on my own. With a few descriptions of some locations, I learned three new locations. There was even time to smell my favorite flowers--lilacs.

Let me be clear: There were some difficulties. Working around food was challenging. I had to be aware of when my dog would need to relieve. I had to get clear directions. I had to educate the public. But I still had fun. Julio still did well. In all, it was a great experience.

Posted by Nickie at 5:26 PM

Saturday, May 21, 2005

Dedication of a dog

Two days ago, I was up REALLY late!! I mean, we're talking past midnight. I had to go to Wal-Mart to get printer ink. We hopped in the car and Mom drove us there. Julio did a pretty good job guiding me. He was sort of distracted, but wouldn't you be at that hour?

I don't like keeping him up that late, but when I do, I make it up to him. He gets lots of pets. I take care of his needs and I try to balance my schedule out so he can rest. It's just something we do for each other: He guides me and I take care of him.

Posted by Nickie at 9:09 PM

Saturday, May 28, 2005

The place for fun in your life

Today Julio, my Grandma, my Mom and I went to a large popular mall. The fact that our weather has been cloudy, sunny, rainy but always constantly cool has prevented people from going camping. So, today, the mall was packed! Tons of kids, parents, couples, teenagers, strollers and adults crowded the walkways and stores. All I needed were a few things. I wasn't feeling all that great at first either.

This scene would be what I refer to as a living hell with a cane. I would have left feeling frustrated. Even if I had gone sighted guide the whole time, the experience would have lacked that fun aspect of independence.

Today, I rarely needed an arm except when we were wandering aimlessly; I didn't want to confuse Julio. Julio did great weaving through pedestrians, stopping for surface and elevation changes, finding escalators and protecting me from strollers pushed by people who didn't see us. It is incredibly fun to see Julio buckle down like this. He was really working. The best part was that he was having fun too! A few distractions did give us some struggles; Julio did pick things up off the floor, occasionally sniff people and get petted which made it hard to continue, but all he needed was a firm "hop up" from me or a correction in the case of a few of the distractions and we were back on the road.

This was one of the rewarding days I love to see when working with a Guide Dog!

Posted by Nickie at 8:05 PM

Sunday, May 29, 2005
Poor boy!

I feel terrible about this: I accidentally caught Julio's tail in the door. The poor boy cried so loud, it was awful! This is the hard part of having a Guide Dog, feeling the pain of another so closely.

Posted by Nickie at 2:16 PM

Friday, July 15, 2005
Graduation

It has been over a month since Julio and I graduated. I'm not sure why it has taken me so long to write in this blog about the experience, but it has. I know that words cannot express how great this experience was. It was dignified and such a treat!

I'll focus on just the day of graduation here, but there was so much more that made the weekend special.

On June 9th, I woke up at 4 AM, even though I'd been up until midnight. I had been working on a paper, but at around midnight, I no longer knew what I wrote. I remember writing about House on Mango Street, then something about starting a guide dog school. So I went to bed and got up at 3:30 or something like that. Needless to say, I was tired. This isn't a good mix for graduation day.

Our class had a rehearsal outdoors. Julio and I practiced as much of the route as many times as we could. I got my cap, gown and tassel. Then did some last minute stuff and headed home. We rigged up a little something to make Julio look like he was part of the class. I had maroon fabric on his harness, and a tassel for it too.

We got things ready then headed out to acupuncture. I had my acupuncture done, and then we went to dinner. I was so nervous! I hardly ate, I was afraid I'd get sick.

Then my friend Marlaina and I went to the rest room. She saw the dress I wore under the gown and told me to quit being nervous.

My mobility instructor and I drove to the school. We had to re-learn things because the ceremony was moved inside.

Now here's the part where the Guide Dog comes in: Julio did not seem to understand the route... At all! I was feeling rushed and pressured and honestly, I was thinking why can't we just go home?

It was hot out and worse in the gym, but I couldn't drink water since there would be no opportunity to use the rest room during the ceremony. My stomach felt awful, and I was exhausted! I thought we'd never get the cue to start the precession!

Finally, we did. I had a good friend in front of me who really helped out. She has a soft voice, which made things challenging, but we made it. Marlaina yelled my name, and that made me smile.

I had to go up twice: once to speak, once to get my diploma. The first time, I went up alone. But there were helpful people nearby. My dean was seated right near the ramp where I needed to go up so he quietly gave me directions like "he's missing it... More right, still more... There!" No one knew. Julio stood by my side for the first little bit, then cracked everyone up by lying down to say "Well, she'll be here a while!"

For the diploma part, the class went up together, and not until we got halfway up the ramp did I walk alone. I did it! No pushing, pulling "Oh my gosh, you're gonna fall!" or anything. Just use of resources like having the photographer and person giving out diplomas say my name. And of course the best guide in the world!

It's so great to have a good, picture perfect memory like this! I've worked hard for it! I really wanted to do it by myself, without help. I didn't want to be the blind girl who needed help to graduate. And with Julio's help, I wasn't. We were a beautiful team!

    Posted by Nickie at 10:58 AM

Julio Blogs

In February of 2006, I realized I needed a guest blogger. The blog needed a new voice, occasionally to tell a different story. So, I "looked the other way", when Julio started using my blog as his own. These are the entries he's written so far.

Heehee
Mar. 29, 2006. 7:09 AM
I hijacked Mom's computer. I'm so wound up; the dorm room can't contain me. Mom's walking too slowly again. And no matter how hard I try, she won't play tug. I don't understand why she gets so mad when I jump and dig my nails into her left foot.

Another day of work for me. Maybe I can get
- A girl to notice me.
- Food off the floor before Mom notices.
- Someone to take me for a run.
- Food off the floor.
- On Mom's bed when she's not looking.
- Food off the floor.

Love,

Julio

PS: Mom says I did a good traffic check. She should give me more food don't you think? My paws are tired, gotta go pester Mom for breakfast.

Oh boy!

Aug. 15, 2006. 11:46 AM

It's me, Julio. I decided to steal Mommy's laptop again (teehee!). Boy, you should've seen me yesterday. Mommy said I did great. We hadn't done any street crossings lately since Mom only started walking half way well last week. Yesterday, I did two of them perfectly; stopped for up curbs and everything!

Today Mommy took me to Target to get some things for the dorm. She got a little chair so she can sit on the floor with me without hurting her butt. It's her favorite, a kind of bluish green color she says. Baxter and I think she should give it to us because it looks so cute.

Mom also got a rug. She said it had to be dark so that if I throw up, the stain might not show as bad. But I'll still get my pretty yellow fur all over it (teehee!).

And, and, and, she got me a new toy, but she says that she can only let me play with it with supervision because I'm not s'posed to have stuffed toys.

She didn't feel up to doing a lot of walking, but I liked the chance to work. I just wish she'd walk faster. And I wish she'd bought me a tall caramel macchiato with whip and cream cheese Danish too. It looked really nummy. Then she got ticked when I tried to vacuum the floor... Sigh.

I sure do love to cuddle with her though. I wonder what she'll get me for my birthday.

Love, hugs, wags and licks!
Julio

Notes of relaxation
Oct. 31, 2006 at 4:59 PM
Hey, it's me: Julio!

Boy was today interesting. We went to that class where Mom lays on the floor in the dark again. First, she did this thing; I think its progressive muscle relaxation, where she tightened and relaxed muscles. That was okay; at least she didn't try it with her left foot this time. She was more awake when she was done with that.

The next exercise was tricky. You're supposed to go to the beach in your imagination. Mom didn't like imagining the sand between her toes, she said that hurts. I helped out by smacking her with my paws, and lying down and conking her on the head with my harness. It was fun!

They do some interesting stretches in there. Mom doesn't understand them. I don't either; it just looks like all those people need to play with me! Mom won't let me go play though.

Mom says the relaxation exercises helped with pain-related nausea at least, and that she felt good energy wise. Well, I gotta go. I just thought it'd be fun to write here again, since Mom says her brain is fried.

Love and licks,
Julio

Food distractions are fun
Feb 17, 2006 at 4:06 PM

It's me, Julio. Man, are food distractions fun! I love it when I can try to grab crumbs off the floor. It's especially fun when I make mom plant her bad foot to keep from doing a nose dive. It's like squeaking a toy... Mom makes the weirdest noises...

Mom says she's really frustrated, and afraid of people thinking she's a bad handler.

But I like her lots. My tummy just gets the best of me. And she has a harder time correcting me when she's using her support cane. Teehee...

We went to Brewberry's today, and there were people who kept saying how cute it was that I wanted crumbs on the floor. I like it when they tell Mom she's wrong.

We're still a good team most of the time. I just get distracted by my labradorable Stomach. Mom gets mad, but when we get home, she still plays with me lots. I wiggle and play with my bones. Then when she's trying to do her relaxation exercises, I jump on the bed and land on her stomach. Then I pin her and give her gobs of kisses.

Well, I better go. Mom will get mad if I slobber all over her laptop. I guess it was a lot of money, so I should be nice. Here are some tail wags.

Clicker training

Kid in a candy store
Mar. 13, 2007 at 6:34 PM

Wow... I know that we will still have bad days as a team, but today was cool. Julio is learning how to target my hand, and has finally decided that "come" is a good four letter word, not a bad one. As soon as I feel the nose on my hand, I click and treat. How cool is it to be looking for opportunities to praise and say "Yeah!!!! That's what I want!" instead of having to correct for sniffing, veering or run after the dog even though you're having an awful pain day.

And, as a bonus, I got to practice a physical therapy exercise (walking backward), while doing this. Julio thought it was a game.

Could clicker training be good for my RSD? Maybe there's more to animal therapy than even I thought. It's too bad my friend couldn't have used this example in her presentation during the holistic therapies course. I have a feeling clicker will be helpful at CSUN next week. I'll shut up now, before I sound like an advertisement.

Who's training who?
Apr. 6, 2007 at 12:53 PM

I'm attempting to teach Julio to target chairs, but can't get him to target the actual chair. He knows to target my hand, but won't target the chair unless that hand is on the chair. Baxter, who was watching me, has figured out what the clicker means, and seems to respond well. He's now figured out targeting chairs somewhat, and was "proffering paws" for clicks. Which dog am I training?

A quick click
Apr. 29, 2007 at 5:28 PM

Today, I think I did something good. I know intellectually about the use of pacing to manage pain. I'm still very high on the pain scale, but I decided that if I don't do something, even if I try to push really hard through all of it, I'm going to be in trouble. Because at some point, my body will give out if I don't give it a break.

So, anyway, I took a short break just now. I was trying to figure out what I could do that was fun and

Nickie's Nook

productive at the same time. So, of course, I grabbed the Clicker and started working with Julio. We've been working on come off leash, which he's gotten pretty darn good at, so today we worked also on heel off leash. Using my hand as a target, I began shaping Julio to heel. And, it was pretty successful.

Certainly, we didn't spend a lot of time on it, but as Karen Pryor (can't remember how to spell her name right now), suggests, I kept it short and successful, and we ended on a high note.

So, I did something good for me and the pup. And that's definitely something for me to click about.

Shape up...
May 31, 2007 at 10:06 PM

Yes, it's me, talking about clicker and how much I love it again. With the help of my family, I was able to shape Julio into two commands in the last three days:

"Give me a paw"

"Give me five."

He would put his paw on you before if you petted him long enough, but he wouldn't do it on command. Give me five is not the same as give me a paw. Giving a paw is with the human hand flat. Give me five is with the fingers pointing upward. Shape one, and shaping the other is easier.

I'll say that it's not easy. You've really got to be in tune with your dog. What signals is your dog giving you? What positive shifts are happening? What can you do to take any frustration away?

I discovered that playing with Julio a certain way got him to lift a front paw. I also noticed that he wasn't confident I would be nice while holding the paw, or that he wouldn't lose his balance. So, I held his paw while he was laying in my lap and clicked, and clicked (always treating, of course). And then I played with him and he put his paw in my flat hand. There were many ideas that didn't work, but after a day, he was providing the behavior on cue pretty well, and by today he really had it.

I then held my hand with fingers pointing up. Julio, knowing that the hand was important smacked his paw pads into my hand (perfect high five after a few tries and realizing I wouldn't click for smacking my arm). Then, while clicking, I said "give me five!"

Then, I backed the cue up until he understands the verbal and visual cue together. It's not necessary to remove either cue, since they are both necessary for the trick.

Why did I teach Julio a trick? Isn't he a guide dog? Because this is a way for me to learn how to teach him better, and it's cute.

What did I learn? To watch for signs of stress. Watch for signs of positive change. Reinforce him for good things and let the bad stuff extinguish itself. And that varying the reward keeps him interested.

A lot of this can be applied to people. Maybe not always with the clicker, but in positive ways of changing behavior and working in a partnership. Somedays, I wish I could write a book about what my guide dog showed me about social work. Maybe that's another blog entry...

Writings I'm especially proud of

CRPS: The Condition of Hell

"If hell was a medical condition, it might look something like Reflex Sympathetic Dystrophy," a respected physician noted (Moskowitz and Lang, 2003). Few people can imagine an injury becoming more painful as time passes; a sprained ankle which should heal within a month swelling to the size of a knee or a hand being ice cold and turning purple. But that is what happens with Complex Regional Pain Syndrome or CRPS (Type I), previously known as Reflex Sympathetic Dystrophy. The disorder effects at least one in 100,000 Americans, but due to mis-diagnosis and poor awareness of the disorder, it is possible that the disorder affects many more (Moskowitz and Lang, 2003). The syndrome is characterized by burning pain, which is considered to be disproportionate to the initial injury. And although CRPS is considered a rare disorder, it is possible that up to 20% of Americans have some form of chronic pain. Because chronic pain affects so many people, it is important to understand CRPS and chronic pain in general. CRPS will be explained through the use of scientific and clinical data and hypotheses, and the language of chronic pain will be explored to more fully understand both the scientific and societal influences and implication for people with CRPS.

CRPS has many officially recognized symptoms and some symptoms that are not recognized officially, but that many CRPS patients describe. The symptom that all physicians who treat this condition recognize though is intense burning pain. Patients frequently experience color changes, excessive swelling (edema), and changes in hair and nail growth of the affected limb. Patients complain of struggling with movement of the effected limb, excessive sweating and muscle spasms. Researchers have found movement disorders and "neglect like" symptoms, in which the limb with CRPS feels foreign to the patient (Galer and Jensen, 1999). These symptoms are generally used to diagnose CRPS, but again, the largest symptom is pain "disproportionate to the inciting trauma".

Despite these objective signs and symptoms, there is no test or lab work which signifies that a patient has CRPS. Doctors generally use their own clinical experience to diagnose CRPS, but often use certain procedures to aid in diagnosis. These procedures include infra-red thermograph to measure the temperature of the affected limb as compared to the unaffected limb, special infusions of a chemical to block sympathetic nerve impulses, and sympathetic nerve blocks, which also serve as a treatment for some patients and will be described later (Harden, 2005).

To fully understand CRPS, it is important to understand pain as it is the most definitive symptom of CRPS. According to the International Association of the Study of Pain, pain is "An unpleasant sensory or emotional experience which we primarily associate with tissue damage or describe in terms of damage, or both" (QTD in. Moskowitz and Lang, 29). For example, the sensation of a burn to the hand after touching a stove is considered pain because it is both unpleasant and is associated with damage to tissue like skin. A commonly understood explanation of acute pain is that pain helps the body protect itself. For example, pain causes a person to remove a hand from a hot stove or avoid walking on a broken leg. The nerve fibers sense the damage and the information passes through the dorsal horn of the spinal column. The brain receives the information, and reacts. There are many possible responses to pain, depending upon the injury. An inflammatory response is likely in the case of an injury. It is thought that an exaggerated inflammatory response may play a role in CRPS.

An inflammatory response is caused by the sympathetic nervous system, and is one reason for the previous, but still common understanding of CRPS as an over-firing of the sympathetic nervous system. The sympathetic nervous system is commonly referred to as the "fight or flight" nervous system. It is involved in controlling more automatic processes in the body such as circulation, breathing and digestion. It reacts in response to stressful situations, of which pain is certainly one. The sympathetic nervous system, having received the impulse warning of pain causes swelling to protect the injured area (Moskowitz and Lang, 21-22).

Although there is not currently a widely accepted laboratory test that can objectively identify CRPS, that day may be coming soon. Scientists have found several biological markers that are present in CRPS. Researchers have found DNA changes in the cells of the spinal cords of CRPS patients (Juris, 11). There is also evidence that a portion of the brain shrinks when the CRPS patient is experiencing significant pain, however that change appears to be reversible (Galer, 2006 P 4).

It is precisely these biological and neurological changes that distinguish CRPS from other chronic pain conditions. Additionally, a condition like back pain remains local and does not usually spread. There may be nerve damage, but the changes are generally limited to the site of original injury, although they can cause pain radiating into a limb. CRPS shows changes in the entire nervous system, such as those associated with a sympathetic response. Research also shows a loss of small nerve fibers in skin biopsies from the affected limbs of CRPS patients (Groopman, 2005.)

Because of the response of the nervous system in CRPS, many doctors felt that CRPS was necessarily degenerative. They believed that CRPS had three or four stages, and that all patients progressed linearly through those stages. The first stage is acute CRPS, stage two is the dystrophic stage, stage three is the atrophic stage and stage four involves the inner organs and treatment with implanted devices is strongly considered (RSD Hope, 2007).

The hypothesis of stages, as with many hypotheses in CRPS, has not been shown to be effective clinically. This hypothesis was created when Complex Regional Pain Syndrome type I was called Reflex Sympathetic Dystrophy.

Doctors commonly find with CRPS that the condition responds very differently between patients who would normally be considered similar in other health classifications. Because of these differences in response to therapies, doctors treat CRPS with numerous medications, procedures and therapies. The Reflex Sympathetic Dystrophy Syndrome Association publishes treatment guidelines which suggest pharmacological management, physical and occupational therapy, psychological interventions and other complementary therapies. The focus of these guidelines is decreasing pain and increasing function (Harden, 2006).

Pharmaceutical interventions are not curative, but do help many patients to recover function. Pain is relieved through analgesics and adjuvant analgesics, meaning medications that are not always used to treat pain. Patients first try to treat their pain with over-the-counter pain medications such as Acetaminophen (Tylenol) or anti-inflammatory such as Ibuprofen. Anti-inflammatory medications relieve pain, but also relieve swelling. While these medications can be enough to control the pain for some patients, not all patients receive enough relief from these medications. Doctors generally try to choose medications that will relieve as much of the pain as possible, and aid a patient in functioning more effectively with the least amount of side effects. For example, a tricyclic antidepressant treats nerve pain by increasing Serotonin and Norepinephrine, but also cause drowsiness and can be helpful for a patient who struggles to sleep because of the pain. An anti-seizure medication like Gabapenten (Neurontin) or Pregabalin (Lyrica) can calm nerve pain, and aid in reducing allodynia or sensitivity to touch and other stimuli which would not normally be painful. Some patients also find relief with a lidocaine patch. Lidocaine is a local anesthetic, which decreases nerve activity and can produce relief.

However, relieving inflammation, calming excited nerves, relieving depression and insomnia, sleeplessness are not always enough to relieve pain enough to help the patient function. Doctors sometimes need to add an opioid pain reliever such as Vicodin or Oxicontin. In this case, doctors try to find a medication which will help the patient's pain, but also avoid side effects such as drowsiness and constipation. When treating a patient with opioids, doctors also must avoid addiction to the medication, although this is generally considered a rare problem when opioids are used to treat pain. Some doctors use contracts which outline patient's and physician's responsibilities (Harden, 2005).

Another tool physicians commonly use is a nerve block. In essence, a nerve block involves injecting medication, usually a local anesthetic, to block nerve transmissions. The most common nerve block used for both the diagnosis and treatment of sympathetically mediated, originating from the sympathetic nervous system, pain in CRPS is a sympathetic nerve block. This is usually done in the neck or in the lumbar spine. The sympathetic nervous system lies on the sides of the spine, so the physician guides a long needle near the spine to block sympathetic activity. A patient can confirm that she or he has received a sympathetic block by the increase in temperature which occurs after the block. This is because the veins dilate and allow more blood to the extremities (Harden, 2005). Though these blocks seem to be less common, I have personally received an ankle block, named because it blocks nerves in the ankle which stops sensation and pain in the foot and an epidural injection which numbs the lower half of the body. There are very few studies on the efficacy of these two injections.

One new treatment which holds significant promise is the ketamine infusion. Ketamine is an anesthetic which blocks chemicals which excite the nervous system. While studies are limited, this particular medication has assisted 85% of patients at one treatment center in becoming more active or reducing their daily medications (Getson, 2005).

Although in depth description of these treatments is beyond the scope of this paper, it is important to know that psychological therapies such as biofeedback, relaxation and coping skills are often used with CRPS patients. Physicians also prescribe physical therapy to aid the patient in strengthening and desensitizing the limb (Harden, 2005).

After understanding the scientific aspects of CRPS, it is important to understand both the societal and literary concepts that affect CRPS and the patients and care givers who experience it. Unfortunately, there is very little popular literature about CRPS. Chronic pain is discussed generally, but CRPS is rarely mentioned, and even more rarely explored in depth.

In the Civil War, one doctor gained experience with CRPS firsthand. S. Weir Mitchell noticed that some of his patients experienced pain long after their wounds and surgical sites had healed. He referred to this nerve pain as "causalgia", which is now considered CRPS type II, which only differs clinically in that it has a definable major nerve injury. Mitchell described the pain of CRPS in Injuries of Nerves and Their Consequences, which is commonly cited in patient information available today. Mitchell described the responses of the soldiers he treated in this way: "Under such torments the temper changes, the most amiable grow irritable, the soldier becomes a coward and the strongest man is scarcely less nervous than the most hysterical girl" (Mitchell,

1872, P 196). While Mitchell's quote demonstrates the sexism of the day, in that crying and screaming are attributed to a "girl", it does demonstrate some compassion for patients with the disorder. It was also the first known discussion of the syndrome.

Mitchell's observations also described the pain as having some sort of pathology, and being directly affected by nerves. This is an important acknowledgement, since society still misunderstands this condition as arising from a psychological disorder (Gayler, 2006. Mitchell, 1872.) As explained earlier, some of this misunderstanding arises from the unique differences between CRPS and other painful conditions, and some is likely due to the co-morbidity of depression and CRPS (Gayler, 2006).

One common misconception about people with CRPS is that all CRPS patients are trying to avoid pain too much. As an unpleasant sensation, pain is something most humans try to avoid at some point, which is the reason for pain. The example of jerking a hand away from a hot stove shows the benefit of this. By jerking a hand away, a person avoids a terrible burn. Doctors who see many people complain of simple sprains may become skeptical of a CRPS patient who legitimately needs relief. Friends and family may believe that the person with CRPS is trying too hard to avoid pain or malingering, when in reality, a CRPS patient experiences much more pain than someone with a simple sprain.

Another common view of people with CRPS is that they suffer from psychosomatic illness. Unfortunately, that view is widespread.

"One common complaint from patients is that their family members do not really believe they are ill and do not understand their pain. In fact, there was a time when many doctors thought RSDS existed only in the patient's head. When a disease is difficult to understand and doctors cannot find a way to treat its symptoms, they often conclude it is a psychosomatic disorder. Physicians are trained to treat illnesses and help their patients. When nothing they do works, they often resort to a psychological diagnosis rather than admit defeat. If doctors have trouble believing their patients' accounts of the pain they experience, it is no wonder that family and friends have the same problem" (Moskowitz and Lang, 2003 P. 124).

As shown in this passage, patients are not only harmed by this attitude from their families and friends, but also their doctors. This can delay treatment and cause the loss of a job or friends. In extreme cases, it can lead to suicide if the patient believes no one will help manage their pain or put together the pieces of the patient's life. The stigma of psychological conditions is a large problem for CRPS patients. Instead of believing that psychological pain is real pain, society tends to use depression or anxiety as reasons to ignore a person's pain. The link between chronic pain and depression is strong. In many cases, friends and family see depression that is caused by chronic pain and assume it is what caused the pain in the first place. The slogan for a commercial for Cymbalta is "Depression hurts." The drug was actually designed to aid in treatment of depression or nerve pain, but the commercial creates the image of depression "causing" pain. While there is a link, it is not nearly what the commercial suggests.

Macdonald (2000) describes current social work practices in chronic pain treatment programs. She explains that pain is defined in three different "cells" in a behaviorist or contingency management model. The first cell describes pain as a "sick role" that is "reinforced" by the patient's environment. The pain may be "real", but it is "psychological" in nature. Usually, patients' lives are analyzed to see if there is some kind of gain for the patient to be sick. A gain might be sympathy, reduced or no work, or any other stimulus or cue perceived as a reward. The treatment is to ignore the patient's "pain behaviors", such as limping, wincing, saying "ouch" or other indications that the patient is in pain. Then, the therapy team reinforces "well" behavior. It is thought that this will restore health to the patient (Macdonald, 2000 P. 52).

Another cell of the contingency management model assumes that pain is biological in nature. This means that pain has pathology, a sprain or strain shows the pathology of stretched ligaments. This might also include pain conditions that currently cannot be detected on x-ray or MRI, since what can be detected medically now is very different from what could be detected twenty years ago, it is possible that pain that seems to have no cause now will be discovered to have a cause in the future. This would be the more scientific explanation of pain. Macdonald explains that "Chronic cancer pain and neurological pain have been traditionally classified in this category, because there is obvious and observable organic damage to explain the pain. The symptomatology specifically fits with the signs of scientifically classified disease processes and therefore is deemed a legitimate concern that elicits medical intervention" (Macdonald, 2000, P. 52). Patients with CRPS sometimes find themselves confused by cell one and cell two, and find it difficult to explain the causation of their pain. I have been told that stress effects my symptoms, and this sometimes leads me to feel that my pain is not legitimate.

Macdonald explains that to meet the needs of a chronic pain patient, it is best to treat the physical pain and provide psychological support to deal with the implications of chronic pain on the life of the "sufferer" (Macdonald, 2000, P. 53). Moskowitz and Lang (2003) explain that treatment for CRPS "consists of three parts. The first is the control of pain by medication and other techniques; the second is psychosocial support and treatment; and the third is functional activation and rehabilitation" (69). This reality is difficult to accept, however, because of the stigma around chronic pain and mental illness. These miss-conceptions must be resolved within the patient, so that healing can take place. A more realistic understanding of the relationship between pain, depression and CRPS could help the patient resolve these challenges.

A common metaphor for bodily processes such as the immune system and medical treatment in general is the metaphor of war. This metaphor has been extended to pain medicine and research. A respected and empathetic pain physician, Scott Fishman, wrote The War on Pain, in which he recounted his experience treating diverse people and their pain. His book also explains quite a bit about various conditions, medications and complementary treatments. He specifically invokes a war metaphor in many of his descriptions. The war metaphor for pain does have some benefits. When pain is so intense that it causes shock, or creates difficulty in day to day life, "fighting" the pain is important. In the forward to Fishman's The War On Pain, Thomas Moore writes "Pacifist that I am, seeped in the unbelligerent imagery of Taoism, I admit that I worry some about his root metaphor of conducting a war on pain" (2). Besides the desire to avoid war, and promote peace, the war metaphor may promote a feeling of futility. With a condition like CRPS, there is often a feeling of failure or losing. This is problematic, not just for people with pain, cancer or AIDS, but also for people with CRPS.

Scientists describe the sympathetic nervous system as the "fight or flight" nervous system. This imagery does make sense from an evolutionary perspective, in which pain is a form of "attack" and one must either fight or leave to survive. The simplistic explanation of CRPS and the one explained most frequently to newly diagnosed patients or simply interested people used to be that the sympathetic nervous system was "overactive" and the "fight or flight" response caused most, if not all, of the pain. This is very similar to the previous descriptions of the immune system "fighting" any invading pathogens. This language is damaging to a patient, who is often told to "fight" a disease. Moskowitz and Lang (2003) explain that an attitude of "I did not ask for this, but I will fight it tooth and nail," [is] harmful and [needs] to be handled with a mental health professional. [A patient] may unconsciously sabotage all ... efforts to deal with the illness. At the very least, [this] reaction will make... efforts to live as well as [possible] less effective. It is important to accept that some things just happen" (108-109). War as a metaphor for treatment of CRPS is counter-productive. Further, because of the feeling of futility that war and battle metaphors create, the patient may attempt to fight harder, and increase both the activity of the sympathetic nervous system and the pain.

Fishman does, however, acknowledge that the war should have limits. "We should never surrender to pain, but neither should we become too entrenched in combat to negotiate a truce. If you've been battling chronic pain, you may be locked in a struggle that's consumed months or years. Life is just too short to remain in a war zone any longer than absolutely necessary" (Fishman, 2005). While declaring a truce is a more helpful image, it still does not encompass all of the experience of a CRPS patient. It sets the patient up for feeling like a failure. Even as I have realized that having CRPS is not my fault and I have not lost the battle, many others feel that I am "not fighting it hard enough". The war metaphor is so prevalent in society that avoiding the "fight or flight" response is nearly impossible.

One of the concepts that complicates society's understanding and doctors' treatment of pain is the concept of pain as an alarm. Many physicians and physical therapists are quick to point out that pain prevents many serious injuries. A person who walks long distances in shoes that do not fit correctly will receive blisters. The pain caused by the blister causes the person to walk less the next day or find shoes that fit and do not cause pain in that spot. In many ways, pain is an alarm. A fire alarm prevents injury by warning that fire, or at least smoke, is in the building. Pain does much the same thing. It is, of course, hard to remember that pain has positive aspects while experiencing severe pain. Many people with even a twisted ankle ask the doctor to relieve or completely remove their pain. In my experience, many doctors are extremely hesitant to do this. When my injury that precipitated the CRPS happened, my doctor encouraged me to let pain be my guide to avoid further injury. My doctor said the same thing after both of my surgeries. Acute pain can literally mean the difference between a small blister and a third degree burn.

Because of the alarm metaphor of pain, many people view pain as a gift. Dr. Paul Brand spent his life working with leprosy patients. He wrote of the struggle many patients experience because they cannot feel. Leprosy can cause a deadening of the nerves. Until relatively recently, doctors thought the condition caused fingers to drop off or shorten. Brand observed that patients actually had injuries that they could not feel. Without pain, they could not easily prevent the injury, or monitor its healing. In The Gift of Pain, he describes how many of the sores, infections, ulcers and shortenings of bones that were once thought to be caused by the disease of leprosy itself are actually caused by injuries which are not prevented by pain. An ulcer could start from a simple painful blister, which would warn a person with a typical amount of sensation and, without thinking about what was taking place in the body; she or he would shift weight, change shoes or take a break. Brand described blisters or even tiny spots of inflammation which created ulcers, and because the patient with leprosy could not feel any pain from the ulcer, the patient never rested or shifted weight. The ulcer never healed and the foot or hand needed to be amputated. "For the first time I noticed something. [The patient] had no limp! I had just spent half an hour cleaning out a grossly abscessed wound on the ball of his foot, and he was putting his full weight on the exact spot we had so carefully treated" (Brand 120). Certainly, this is a valid reason to appreciate pain. Pain aids in preventing and healing injuries. My personal experience has generally shown two responses to this. Some sincerely want to never experience pain. They do not feel satisfied if a doctor does not completely eradicate their pain. Others see pain as a gift and cannot understand why others need relief. This second general group tends to be the group of people who do not believe that CRPS exists, or they create causation of the pain and thus, the condition.

Brand wrote of a woman whom experienced CRPS in such a light. Her CRPS developed after an operation which required her to keep her arm in an uncomfortable position for three weeks. By the time she visited Brand, the woman was incredibly angry with her original surgeon who had ignored her pain. She had an advanced case of CRPS. Though the chapter in which Brand describes her case is entitled "Intensifiers of Pain," he also states causation "I concluded the woman had lost use of her hand because of anger and distress. I could find no other physiological cause" (Brand, 268). Certainly, anger does increase sympathetic nervous system activity; however, it has already been shown that CRPS is not always sympathetically maintained. This implied causation is harmful to any patient, with any condition. Like the war metaphor, it places the burden mostly on the patient. While a patient must take responsibility for his or her own recovery, these metaphors do not usually point out beneficial areas of responsibility, rather, they waste the patient's time, chasing after problems and societal ideologies that rarely benefit in the long run.

Since there are so many unhelpful metaphors that do not fully or accurately describe the experience of a person with pain, it is important to examine both the metaphors used by and the lived experiences of people with pain. One reason pain is so poorly understood by society, besides the obvious biological complexities of pain, is that people with pain struggle to explain their own narratives. "Narrative conventions call for coherence; stories should integrate life experiences and create a whole. For chronic pain sufferers that seems to be a challenging task, for if pain continuously destroys or threatens the self and the world then every narrative of the self in pain remains fragile" (Becker, 1999). This passage appeared in an article discussing pain in later life. It portrays the challenge of describing the experience of pain and its effect on the person. Indeed, I have personally experienced the fragileness of my own sense of self. Writing this paper, and portraying my experiences and those of others with pain has been one of the most challenging writing projects I have ever participated in. Indeed, my experience of writing about or talking about CRPS and living with pain has felt fractured and fragile. Others also embody this fragility and sense of a fractured narrative. As Brand described her, the woman he operated on whom CRPS had told her story in such a way that he struggled to understand what had happened to cause her pain (Brand 268). For this woman, pain stole her sense of self. She could not release her anger because her pain remained unrelieved.

Pain not only destroys the sense of self and the ability to construct a narrative, by its nature, it prevents a narrative from being formed. In "Pain: The Disease," Elaine Scarry explained "pain is not a linguistic experience; it returns us to the world of cries and whispers. Patients grope at far-fetched metaphors" (Thernstrom, 2001). Concrete descriptions of pain are challenging, because many times, a patient does not actually know what pathology is causing the pain. Even when a condition like CRPS is diagnosed, few people have experienced or identified this type of pain. A vivid description such as "it feels like my leg is on fire", is an experience few people are unfortunate enough to have.

Most CRPS patients have probably not experienced the concrete version of the metaphor.

Fortunately, there are metaphors that can be easily understood and pictured by others. They may not always describe the pain itself, but they can portray the experience of living with pain. "Chronic pain is like water damage to a house—if it goes on long enough, the house collapses. By the time most patients make their way to a pain clinic, it's very late," Dr. Daniel Carr, director of the pain clinic at the New England Medical Center explained (Qtd. in Thernstrom, 2001). This metaphor describes the experience of a person with chronic pain, its effect on a person's life, without placing burden only on the shoulders of the patient. It avoids the guilt that is so often present in descriptions of pain. Water damage to a house usually invokes compassion. No one would say "if you only tried harder, you would not have had that flood last year."

It is important to remember that describing pain has implications beyond explaining CRPS to friends, family and strangers who cannot understand why a young woman or man is using a cane, wheelchair or walker, or why a patient is wearing gloves on a hot but windy day. It is also important that doctors be able to understand the quality and quantity of a patient's pain to either diagnose a patient's condition or track the progress of treatment. Fortunately, doctors can choose among several methods to evaluate pain. One such method, the McGill Pain Index relies on the language of pain and indirectly relies upon some of the metaphors described above. The index uses a questionnaire in which patients describe their pain's qualities by choosing words from various groups. The groups allow physicians to see a pattern in the type of pain that is described. "Pain is scaled in four categories: sensory, affective, evaluative, and miscellaneous. Affective words would include `exhausting,` `frightful,` `vicious,` and `torturing.` Sensory words would include `throbbing,` `aching,` `dull,` `stabbing,` and `piercing.` Evaluative words would include `mild,` `excruciating,` and `agonizing" (Moskowitz and Lang, 55). These groupings can create helpful dialogue about the pain, and even with a patient who has seen a particular physician for years, the groupings can provide information about which treatments might still be needed. Certainly, they give a patient a general idea of where to start to describe the pain. I personally found that this questionnaire helped me to know how to talk with family members and friends.

The authors of the scale also created a chart to demonstrate the intensities of various pain conditions. Causalgia, the name used with CRPS Type II ranks at the top of the scale. To help the general public and doctors who are unfamiliar with the conditions described, the authors compared the pain conditions to child birth and accidents. CRPS ranked above forty on the scale, which is comparable only to amputation of a finger (Juris, 149).

One other method of describing the quantity of pain is using the ten point scale. A patient is asked to rate the pain on a scale of zero to ten, where zero is no pain and ten is the worst possible pain. The idea is that this gives the patient a good way to tell the physician how much pain she or he is in. In reality, a ten point scale cannot possibly convey pain fully. I experience many types of sixes on the pain scale. I also find that my concept of the scale changes. What I thought of as an eight one year ago, I would now view as a four. This does give my doctor and I somewhere to start, however. With practice, I have learned to translate the language of pain in words such as "ouch" or "it hurts" to more descriptive phrases like "I am at a nine on the pain scale. This thunder storm is making my pain increase. Mostly, it is burning, but there is some electrical shock like pain and quite a bit of aching." This new language, combined with the more helpful metaphors and thought about narrative can help to create a better meaning for the pain of CRPS.

While CRPS can be both physically and emotionally devastating to a patient, and can indeed feel like "hell", war or a collapsing house, scientists and physicians are making progress. Patients can, in many cases, retain and regain function. Metaphors and narratives can adjust to promote healing. A CRPS sufferer can regain a sense of self and the house of her life can be rebuilt.

Works Cited

Fishman, Scott, and Lisa Berger. The War on Pain. Harper Paperbacks, 2001.

"Four Stages of RSDS." American RSD Hope. 2007. 10 May 2007 <http://www.rsdhope.org/showpage.asp?PAGE_ID=5>.

Galer, Bradley S. "Complex Regional Pain Syndrome:." RSDSA. 2006. 5 May 2007 <http://www.rsds.org/3/education/galer_2006.htm>.

Getson, Philip. "Overview of Ketamine Infusion Therapy." RSDSA. 2007. 13 May 2007 <http://www.rsdsa.org/3/treatment/ketamine.html>.

Groopman, Jerome. "When Pain Remains." The New Yorker 10 Oct. 2005: 36-41. Academic Search Premier. Ebsco. College of St. Catherine, St. Paul.

Harden, Norman. "Complex Regional Pain Syndrome: Treatment Guidelines." RSDSA. 2005. 5 May 2007 <http://www.rsdsa.org/3/clinical_guidelines/index.html>.

Juris, Elena, and Edward Carden. Positive Options for Reflex Sympathetic Dystrophy. Alameda: Hunter House, 2005.

Moskowitz, Peter, and Linda Lang. Living with RSDS. Oakland: New Harbinger Publications, Inc., 2003.

Thernstrom, Melanie. "Pain: the Disease." New York Times 16 Dec. 2001. 6 May 2007 <http://query.nytimes.com/gst/fullpage.html?Sec=health&res=9C02E4DD163FF935A25751C1A9679C8B63>.

Yancey, Philip, and Paul Brand. The Gift of Pain. Grand Rapids: Zondervan, 1997.

Never Forsaken

The summer of 2004 was the busiest summer I've experienced. It's not unusual for a seventeen-year-old girl to spend some time away from the family either at a camp or on vacation with friends, but it's not usual for one to spend seven weeks away from home, family and friends. Because I attended a blindness convention and a training program to learn skills I'd need to live independently, I'd already spent three weeks away from home by the time I left to train with my Guide Dog, Julio. This story begins at the training program and then follows me to guide dog training. It tells of how I experienced the love of God even in some trying and scary times.

People might wonder why the Guide Dog school had concerns about my training. Guide Dog training is physically, mentally and emotionally strenuous. The cost of training a Guide Dog team in 2004 was about $46,000. My instructors needed to make sure that I would be able to safely finish the training. Now that I have worked with Julio for two years, I understand their actions.

"There's a note in your pouch," my teacher said as I entered the basement of the dormitory.

"About what?" I wondered. I walked to the wall that held pouches containing a card with a record of where we'd been and a label in Braille so we could find it ourselves. I snatched the card from my pouch. My fingers trembled as I read it.

"Your parents will pick you up at 7:20 tomorrow for a doctor's appointment," the note read.

"Did they say what for?" I asked.

"You need to get okayed for Guide Dogs, maybe you should just call one of them and ask."

I slid the note into my pocket and ran upstairs. My heart pounded, more from fear than cardiovascular exertion. Why do I need to go to the doctor? I already passed the home interview and I have my plane ticket. I was up front about my tendonitis, even before I knew what it was. Why are they concerned about it now?

I shoved open the door to the room I shared with two other blind high school students and threw my cane into a corner.

My mind began to trick me; I believed something sinister was going on. I dialed our voice mail at home to see if there were any messages from the school. There were none.

I called my mother on her cell phone and demanded to know what was going on. She tried to calm my fears, but I wasn't listening.

"You should've told me! Why didn't they talk to me?" Mom tried to explain that they didn't want me to worry. She knew how important getting a Guide Dog was to me.

"You're busy. We didn't want you to worry about this too. We hoped you wouldn't have to know."

"Well, I do," I shouted into the phone. "I have to go," I said cutting her response off. I hung up without saying "I love you."

I heard my roommates in the room now, but I ignored them. I walked to the bathroom as quickly as I could, without bumping into walls. I wanted to be alone. I cried so hard I couldn't talk. I left the room without saying a word to anyone.

Downstairs, I talked to my teacher. We'd known each other for five years; she's seen me go through a lot of hard times. She helped me prepare to get a Guide Dog. I knew she'd understand.

Other adults gathered as we talked and many of them reassured me. "It's not a matter of if, it's when," they said. But that wasn't what I wanted to hear. I wanted to fight back. I was angry with my parents for not telling me, and I hated the thought that people talked about me without my knowledge. Eventually I collected myself enough to help prepare dinner and join my friends. But that night a panel of blind adults shared their experiences with us; two of them had Guide Dogs. Students naturally asked about them and I could barely stand listening to the explanations of how they worked. That could've been me. But now it won't be.

The next morning the doctor said I needed an evaluation to make sure I could handle the walking. "I think you'll be fine, but we need to make sure," he said. Maybe this can work, I hoped.

I went through the evaluation easily. The walking didn't cause more pain so they concluded I would be fine. Thank You God! I prayed.

A week later, after three days of learning how to use a Guide Dog, the instructors told the class about our dogs. Mine was a yellow lab named Julio. I practically skipped back to my room to wait to meet him; I always wanted a yellow lab.

Finally an instructor walked me to the room where I met him. One of the instructors described him to me.

"Did you tell her about his eyes?" one of the other instructors asked.

"They're beautiful. They are dark and expressive. They look like someone put eye liner on them." Those will be my eyes, I thought.

We spent the next week learning to work with each other. I struggled with being pulled around obstacles by a dog who couldn't tell me what he was doing; I couldn't tell whether he was moving to the left to keep me away from a signpost or to chase a squirrel. Finally one day I thought I was succeeding. We were really communicating.

"We're going to do a bus to lounge today," an instructor explained. "We're going to park the buses somewhere and tell you how to get to the lounge. Then you're going to get there with us watching. We'll help you if you need us, but we want you to try as much yourself as possible." Oh no! I'm really going to mess this up, I thought.

The wait on the bus lasted 15 minutes, but to me it seemed longer. My classmates told me I'd be fine, but I disagreed.

When it was my turn to go I fought to clear my mind. How am I going to do this? I can't even think straight. I grabbed Julio's harness and took off down the sidewalk. My first street crossing went well; this isn't so bad, I thought. But when we arrived at the next crossing we couldn't get it right. We veered to the left and had to try it several times. After the third try I wanted to curl into a ball and cry. I want to go home and forget the last two weeks ever happened, I thought. But I couldn't; by this time two instructors were trying to help me and I didn't want to look immature.

Finally we got it right and walked on. Both of us felt awful. Julio knew I was upset; he walked at a snail's pace. We walked the rest of the route with little difficulty; Julio even protected me from a car in a driveway.

I still wanted to go home, though. God, why did you bring me here? Do you want me to leave? I figured if I listened to Him, He had an answer.

"I brought you here. I didn't do it to leave you. You went through the uncertainty two weeks ago so you would trust me. I will never leave you or forsake you. I will get you through this."

The next morning I felt better; I was still frustrated, but I didn't want to leave.

On August 21, Julio and I graduated from Guide Dogs for the Blind. When they officially presented me with Julio I said a few thank yous, but I knew there were more that I didn't say. That night before I turned out the light, I prayed with gratitude "Thank You God for never leaving me."

An Unseen and Unknown Hero: The Guide

One of three graduation speeches delivered June 8, 2005

Parents, hard classes, sickness, dirty laundry, people who stand in the middle of the hall ... obstacles... We all face them. Even after graduation we aren't exempt from obstacles and challenges. In life we don't often see obstacles before we face them. I don't see obstacles, even those obvious to the rest of you. I collect ways to get around obstacles and deal with them once I hit them; my favorite is using a guide.

We need guides. I'm fortunate, I have several. The one by my side now is Julio. But the kind of guides we need are those who care, know about pitfalls and help us get around them. Guides can be parents, teachers, faith, or friends. These guides help because they know what we go through. They know what always trips us. They remind us that what we're about to do didn't work last time and we'd be wise to avoid it. They warn us when we are being obstacles to ourselves with thoughts starting with "I can't." They catch us when we fall.

Julio is a great guide. Having someone who sees the problem and helps you avoid it is good. Luckily, my guides don't just guide around physical obstacles. They are friends who see me run myself down and refuse to let me continue. Others see something bigger than I can handle and do not let me fight it alone. When I got Julio, my friend Marlaina knew I'd struggle with the stress of Guide Dog school. She called to see how I was and helped keep my spirits high. After you graduate you'll still have guides to help you with hard things in life like the stress of college or a new job.

People aren't the only guides we have. We can also use experiences. I came to this school thinking I could do everything myself and never ask for help. That attitude got me a D plus average in Algebra II. As awful as that was, I learned that I can't always do everything myself and it's okay to ask for help. Hopefully, I'll have the wisdom to remember this in the future. You have experiences like this you can use.

Be warned, guides have caveats. You need guides who know how to handle obstacles -- which to go around and which to go over. One day, Julio and I were walking in the street. We came to a car, but Julio didn't show it to me. He can't go around cars until I tell him to; I had to make him show me. Instead, he jumped landing all four feet on the hood of the car. Needless to say, in this case it was better not to follow. Guides can be wrong by telling you about obstacles you don't need to avoid or not telling you about ones you should. Past experiences are good guides, but don't be limited by them. So what if you did poorly in something before. You can improve in that area. Julio hasn't jumped on the hood of a car since.

Don't become completely distrustful of your guides either. I can't count the times someone told me about stairs in front of me. "Okay," I'd say... Then promptly fall down those stairs. In this case, it's not my guide's fault. Guides cannot protect us forever, especially when we will not listen. Even when we mess up, guides can help. They console us. When I fall down those stairs, my guide still helps me find a band-aid to patch up a scrape or if it's Julio, lick it.

I know we're all excited to get our diplomas and party. But as you continue to face obstacles, think about and thank the guides in your life. They aren't done helping you yet.

Brewberry's on a Sunday Morning

Brewberry's is a local coffee shop near my college. The best description I've heard is that it's like Cheers without the alcohol.

The foot wake up system went off at 5:30 this morning. I didn't want to get up. I lazed around and put away the remaining clean laundry from last Sunday, then sorted the dirty laundry on my floor into light and dark loads. At 7:30 I made my way over to the Coeur De Catherine. St. Kate's is still sleeping; hardly anyone was out. I saw one person who said good morning. The crisp air bit into me as I walked over to Brewberry's on this fall morning. Julio was on his best guiding behavior. He guided me smoothly around all of the pedestrians who walked silently by us. A squirrel scampered above our heads, Julio looked up curiously, but a gentle "hop up" got him going. I didn't really have the pain tolerance to get over here, but somehow, I found some extra. By the time I reached the intersection to cross, the cool stillness had calmed my spirit. Julio made an absolutely perfect left turn so we could cross. His guide work was absolutely flawless across the street; we reached the curb before I could even get nervous and he stopped to show it to me. Someone opened the door for me and I smiled. Julio overshot the door again and brought me to the window, so the audible cue was just what I needed. The Acoustic Sunrise played over the radio. I was the only one here. I got my coffee and muffin and sat down. People arrived slowly still in a sleepy Sunday mood. Now, small groups of people sit at tables, adults work on their laptops or read their newspapers, lingering over their coffee. People come in and say hi; I've talked to them before and they know my name. They remind me of theirs too without being asked. The kids color or talk to their parents. Conversations start; people joke with each other freely, but a serious conversation can start too. I smile and contemplate ordering hot chocolate for the road. Someone calls this the Brewberry's time warp. I call it "going home away from home."

    The walk back was peaceful too. Some would jokingly call this "The Church of the Holy Coffee Cup," I'm not so sure it's a joke though. I don't have a church down here, and these walks are great times for me to talk to God and absorb the peace He gives. It helps me get my heart ready for the day. I don't know how to explain it, but it gives me peace.

A Work Of Art

In spring 2006, I faced many pressures. A large course load and worsening pain levels seemed to squeeze me. I needed to make several decisions. This nun's story was a source of deep comfort.

In theology yesterday, the professor said something interesting. She told us about a sister who had been told to go get a master's degree, but didn't enjoy studying. The nun decided that if she had to get this degree, she was going to take one fun class. She took ceramics and every Wednesday night, she'd go happily to that class. She said that that class was her way of doing theology.

One day, this sister came back, covered in mud from her work with the clay. On this particular night she said something interesting. "The Creator shapes the pot from inside," she told our professor.

This story has created in me a need for reflection. I took a ceramics course in tenth grade. Unexpectedly, it was one of the harder courses I've taken; I was not good at it at all, but I learned a few things about clay. What she says is true. The pressure from inside is what makes the pot and gives its shape, but without the proper support system on the outside, the pot would be nothing but a flat piece of clay with tears in it.

These truths aren't just true in pottery with clay. We have a great Potter who is shaping us. We are vessels of clay, learning and growing into a relationship with God. I've started to see how this pressure is applied in my own and others' lives. Sometimes, it's applied in the form of the pain I experience daily, a really bad flare up, a hard test, a bad route with Julio, a paper I can't understand or a dark night when I feel worthless and alone. These things all shape me, they are pressures.

Pressures are painful, but they bring changes. These things force me to examine priorities, stay in touch with God and find new ways of support. God, like a good potter, knows everything about me. A good potter can tell how the clay is responding to her touch. The potter modifies the pressure accordingly.

God is much like that. He is hollowing us out, making more room for Himself. He applies the right amount of pressure to make us grow, but provides the right amount of support to keep us upright. When, like this week, I am stressed out, nervous and in pain, I can remember who is in control. Then, when I do this, I can focus on the empty spot in me and invite God into my heart and share more fully in what He has for me.

Ablism In Healthcare

This was written as part of the first annual Blogging Against Dis/Ablism Day on May 1, 2006.

Going to the doctor is almost sure to raise many people's blood pressure. It's hard to want to go where you know there are needles and all sorts of other things that will ultimately help you, but may be unpleasant at the time. If it's a new doctor to you, you're probably going to be worrying about how his or her bedside manner is and whether she or he will take your symptoms seriously. But if you have a disability, you can add several other concerns to the list. The problem is, whether intentional or unintentional, ablism happens in the medical community.

I've dealt with chronic pain for three years. Reflex sympathetic dystrophy combined with a flexible foot causing several tendon problems have baffled several doctors as to what may be wrong with me or what they can do. Consequently, I've experienced more than a normal teen's amount of visits to the doctor. What follows is a little of what I've seen in medicinal situations relating to a patient's experience when that patient happens to have a disability. Mainly, these three problem areas fall under the categories of missing confidentiality, missing the point and missing access. After seeing the nasty stuff, we'll try to look at what can be done to change it.

Missing Confidentiality

Let's start with scheduling the first visit. I pick up the phone and dial the office. Most likely, I get an automated menu and get to choose which group of people I want to talk to. I push the corresponding button and am put through to the right person; well, okay, first I'm put on hold, but you get the picture. I answer the questions I need to about reason for visit, name, address and phone number. The person scheduling my appointment offers to give me directions and the call is over. No problem right? Not necessarily; the directions probably aren't much help if they tell me to look for the green roof. But it's possible to ask lots of questions and make my way to the doctor.

Having scheduled the appointment and marked it down in my planner, I make arrangements for transportation to the office. Most of the time, they're not on bus lines or there's something unsafe about the route to get there, so my Mom or Dad gets to come with me. Once I arrive, I check in with the receptionist. Remember that this is my first visit? Here's where the fun starts. I get a stack of forms to fill out. These forms are in print, remember? Since Mom's with me, she gets to fill out the information for me. It's just assumed that this is okay with me. What's the problem with this situation?

Mom and I sit down and start to fill out the form:
Name:
Address:
Phone number:
Emergency contact:
Birth date:
Please check any of the conditions you have:
High blood pressure
Heart disease
Diabetes ETC...
History:
Are you currently sexually active?
Do you take birth control?
Do you have an IUD?

Do you have any of the following STD's?

Have you ever taken any of the following street drugs?

Now do you see the problem? I've never had a situation where I needed to lie on this form, but let's say I'd been a bit less discriminating the weekend before. I now have to tell my mother this, even though I may not be ready or willing to. Leave all judgments as to whether I should tell her at the door because they're irrelevant. With all of the stuff about HIPAA's protection of health information, I'm forced to reveal this to my mother and my health information is no longer between me and my doctor. Further, I'm filling this form out in the lobby. As quiet as I try to be, it's very possible that Joe across the narrow aisle just heard about any of these things. How honest do you really expect me to be about anything if I'm concerned about this information getting out?

I've been put in some awkward positions because of this. I don't really feel comfortable answering questionnaires about my mental or physical health in the lobby. There was the time I had to fill out a depression screening; I didn't know who was around. This was in my college's health center, so for all I knew, a professor I might end up working with could be in the room. While I know and believe that depression is not something to be ashamed of, I think that any of said issues should remain private unless I choose to disclose them. Some questions could be damaging to a student's relationship with a professor if taken out of context. Another time, Mom and I were filling out a form which asked about drug habits. One of the questions asked about whether I had a DUI; we both started laughing. That was slightly awkward.

Missing the Point

Once I'm back in the doctor's examining room, I sometimes face another form of ablism. Luckily, I've been able to minimize my experiences of this sort by finding doctors I feel comfortable with and who treat me with respect. Still, I have experienced this before and will probably experience it again. My chief health complaint has been my foot for three years. My visual impairment (until recently) was very stable and should be a non-issue. But sometimes doctors seem to only focus on my vision issues. Most of the questions seem to be about how much I can see or how I do some random task. Sometimes I'm willing to be helpful and educate anyone who asks, but if my doctor has limited time with me, how do I know that I'm getting the best care possible and that my care isn't being sacrificed to learning more about my vision? If 10 minutes are spent on my blindness (which I'm not even requesting medical care for), and five minutes are spent on my pain and I don't even get to ask all my questions, then I would say my care has been sacrificed. Like I said, this hasn't happened very recently.

Missing Access

Finally, I've gotten through the paperwork and the medical interview, but there are more issues to deal with. It would take a whole book to write about all of them, but to simplify this blog post and write about something I actually understand, I'm going to focus on only one more. Now that my doctor and I have made a plan for treatment, it is my duty to participate in the plan. I can't do that effectively, however, without access to information. It's too easy to hand me a piece of paper and have me make a follow-up appointment in four weeks. Usually, someone reads the paper to me, and if I'm lucky, I get a demonstration of any new procedures I'm supposed to perform. But what if I can't remember what side effects to watch out for? Why does it have to be my mom's responsibility to read the information off the sheet for me? Since these papers usually contain handwriting, it's difficult to have an Optical Character Recognition program convert them into computerized text. This is definitely not the fault of the doctors and nurses I see. They try their best to help me with the information. But this is where technology could play a significant role in the process. Ah, but I'm getting ahead of myself.

If all of this is making your head spin, or you're part of the healthcare industry and wondering if I'm out to get you, don't worry. I don't believe in writing two pages of criticism and not giving suggestions. Let's look at each situation with a different set of eyes.

Keeping It to Ourselves

There are several ways to solve the problem of paperwork. I don't know that we're here yet, but eventually, hopefully, we'll see web-based systems for scheduling appointments. I think it would solve more than one problem to allow patients to fill out paperwork before they come to the doctor. First, from an ablism perspective, as long as some basic standards are followed, a screen reader or magnification program can access the information. Now, that information will stay confidential. I don't know as much about programs to aid people with impairments that affect their hands, but I know they exist. Someone with this type of impairment could fill out their paperwork this way as well. This would have benefits for others without disabilities as well. Patients could take their time answering the questions and give the needed information more accurately and clearly. Doctors could have access to the information in a more readable format (no struggling to read a patient's handwriting). In the meantime, people that schedule appointments could ask if the patient will need any accommodations. This is where you find out about sign language interpreters, interpreters for other languages and issues accessing print information. It's an easy opening which then allows for time to figure out how to handle any issues that may come up. Could work be delegated slightly differently so that someone could read the form to the visually impaired person? If the patient is willing to have someone who is with them fill out the paperwork, could they be given a more private place to work?

People First, Disabilities Later

With the doctor spending too much time on my disability, it may help for me to explain more about what I mean. I don't mind some questions about my disability; I understand curiosity and that there are reasons for asking these questions. I do mind my disability being the focus of an appointment that has nothing to do with my disability. I also understand that sometimes things that don't seem related to me may be huge medically. A short explanation that tells me those questions could actually be related to my current medical concern would go a long way to easing my fears that my concern isn't being addressed. If you're trying to make conversation, remember that I'm much more than a disability. I have many of the same experiences as any other college student. What would you ask about if I didn't have a disability? Remember, too, that if I'm seeing you for an earache that makes me nauseous, I'm probably more concerned about not throwing up in the next two seconds than I am about telling you about my Guide Dog.

A Little Creativity Goes a Long Way

In regards to the difficulties I have accessing information I'm given, there are creative ways to handle it. As more systems move to electronic information, I hope there will be more ways to access that information. Instead of handing me a printed copy of the medical information, maybe it could be emailed to me. Maybe it's already online at a web address I can access when I get home. Or maybe there could be some agreements between organizations that braille material for people with visual impairments and medical establishments. Sometimes, these agencies will email information that was previously in print. That saves money on paper. This is where creativity comes into play.

The Method

Lastly, a few words about methodology. If I've learned anything from psychology and sociology, I've learned that it's important to evaluate possible flaws or shortcomings in method or research. The main shortcoming of this information is that it doesn't address nearly enough of the problems faced by people with disabilities. I can only speak to my own experiences. I don't know nearly enough about other disabilities, ablism or healthcare. I hope you'll take the time to read other blogs, read other stories and learn more. I also hope you'll share your stories with me.

Context

It's important to keep in mind the context in which I offer all of the above remarks. I talked about barriers to access, not necessarily the attitudes which foster them. Women in the feminist movement had to address both the attitudes and the access barriers they faced. I chose to address the barriers to access because while I have my own theories about what attitudes foster ablism, I can't speak for others. My hope in writing this essay was not to be the end-all answer to ablism in healthcare or to address the attitudes which foster it. My goal was to point out a few areas where access is unfairly impaired on the basis of disability. My other hope is that if you're part of the healthcare community, you'll think about these barriers and examine your attitudes toward disability. Hopefully, I've done what I set out to do.

Please share comments about your experiences with me.

The New Empowered You

Dedication

This short story is dedicated to all of the people who came before me, the people who fought for equal rights for people with disabilities. Although Maria experiences discrimination because of her disability, this is now illegal. Just because it is illegal, however, does not mean people do not discriminate.

Still, the work of many people has made my life easier.

Also, it is dedicated to my parents, my sisters (both literal and symbolic), other family and friends for believing in me.

"You be careful out there, Maria. I know you'll do great on that interview." Florence is my favorite cab driver. She is one of those forty-year-old black ladies who care about all her passengers like they are her kids, but she is not overbearing or mean about it. "You behave yourself, you hear." Florence handed me my bag.

"I'm not too good at that," I smirked.

"Lord, don't I know it!"

"Can I help you, sweetheart?" A man's voice asked. I hate it when people call me sweetheart. I am a twenty-four-year-old woman, fresh out of school with a doctorate in psychology.

"Yes, can you tell me if there are any curb-side check-in people available?" I felt the man's hand on my arm. He started pulling. I dropped my Guide Dog Coco's harness and followed. Coco walked along, bewildered.

"Sir, you can just tell me where they are, my dog and I can find them from there."

"Oh, no, I don't mind helping a bit." He did not ask whether I minded his help.

"She needs your help," the man said to someone. "Maybe you'd better call for a wheelchair."

"I'm fine without one, thanks." I turned to the man; "I can take it from here." Luckily, he left.

"May I see your ticket, Ma'am?" The woman sounded young.

"Sure, here it is. I'm going to Boston."

"Very good. Do you need a meet-and-assist?"

"Yes, but tell them not to bring a wheelchair."

"Certainly. Please wait here. I'll send someone."

"Could you ask them to identify themselves?"

"Of course."

"Thank you!" It might sound trivial, having someone identify themselves, but if I am going to walk somewhere with someone, I want to know who they are and that they are an employee with the airport. I had only been standing there for five minutes when I felt someone grab my arm.

"Here's the wheelchair. Now if you'll just be a good girl and sit in it, I'll have you to your gate in no time." I thought I told them to not bring the wheelchair.

"Ma'am, I don't need a wheelchair."

"Of course you do. You're blind."

"I can walk just fine. I have my Guide dog and two healthy legs. If you can just walk along with us, we'll get there quickly."

"All right. I suppose it won't hurt to let you have your way." This went much better than I had expected.

Sometimes, I cannot convince them that I do not need a wheelchair.

"This way, doggy... Come on, this way."

"You can just tell me left or right."

We got through security relatively painlessly. The security people did not distract Coco from her job and they did not ask me to remove her harness. They just let me do my job.

When we got to the gate, the meet-and-assist person spoke with the gate agent. "You take good care of her." I sighed inwardly. I could smell coffee and wanted a latté. I did not expect the gate agent to let me go get coffee. Usually, these employees think they have to baby-sit us too.

"She looks like she can take care of herself."

The meet-and-assist person offered to stay with me. I declined her offer as gracefully as I could, then when I was sure she was a safe distance away, I left in search of coffee. I found the coffee shop with ease, ordered my latté and returned to the gate to drink it.

I even had time to use the restroom before the flight. The gate agent said I could wait for her to get everyone else on the plane then she could help me, but I told her I could do it myself as long as I pre-boarded.

"Good. I figured you could handle it, but I thought I'd ask. It makes my job easier," she laughed. I smiled. For once, someone listened to me. "I'm just about to start pre-boarding. If you give me your ticket, I'll check you in first. OOPS! Looks like you're not in bulkhead. We're full there. Want me to upgrade you to first class?"

"That would be helpful."

"Your dog doesn't look like she wants to curl under a coach seat. Here's your ticket. Door's to your left. Have a good flight."

"Thanks! Coco, forward." I waved at the gate agent then headed to my seat.

One of the flight attendants intercepted me. "May I see your ticket? I can help you find your seat."

"Thank you!" I handed her my ticket.

"Would you like to take my elbow? It might be easier for me to guide you there." I was shocked. Most people will just grab my arm, like the man who helped me find the agent who checked me in at the curb.

"Sure." She guided me to my seat, asked if I needed anything else then left telling me someone would be back to explain emergency procedures shortly.

"Oh, you're beautiful. What a pretty puppy. Are you taking good care of your owner? Yes, that's a good girl." I felt a hand reach between my legs to stroke Coco.

"Please don't do that."

"I know I'm not supposed to pet her, but I just can't help myself. You don't mind."

"Actually, I do. She needs to work. She needs to stay calm. She can't do her job while you're petting her." I did not mention that I hated having someone reach between my legs to pet my dog. The person left.

"Isn't it so nice that they have dogs for people like you? You can go places now." This person never introduced herself. I did not know who she was. "I'll bet you love being out and about." I wanted to tell her that I had been a successful independent person before I got Coco and I would be a successful person long after she died. I was tempted to be sarcastic with her and tell her it was amazing, I could actually use the bathroom now that I had Coco; I didn't have to wear diapers. Instead, I settled for a much calmer approach.

"Yes, she's a great dog. But I can do everything I want to do even if she isn't with me."

"You just keep plugging on." The woman left and I heard someone kneel down in the aisle.

"Okay, sweetie. I'll tell you what to do in case of an emergency." I wondered if there was a toddler on board by the way she said this. But I soon figured out that she was talking to me. She patted my head and grabbed my hand. "Now, sweetie, if you hear us say to get in the crash position, you just tuck your head down and grab your knees. And if there's a loss of pressure, a little mask will come down and you just cover your mouth and nose with it and put the band behind your head. The exit is behind you. Okay, honey?"

"Sure, I've flown before."

"Now, if you need any help, you just let me know."

Soon, the plane was soaring through the sky and so were my hopes for the future. I thought about all of the work I'd done. I'd tried to go into nursing school, but no one thought I could do it. I applied to forty-two colleges and none of them would accept me. But I still wanted to help people. I knew I could do anything I wanted to do, but I didn't want to fight too many battles. Then, I broke my leg. That ended my nursing aspirations. Nursing takes a lot of standing and walking, but my leg didn't heal properly, so I could not be on my feet all day. That made my decision easy; I would scratch nursing school. I decided instead to go into psychology. I figured I could help heal the mind and heart even if I couldn't heal the body.

When I made the decision to be a psychologist, people said it was a good thing. They said they'd never trust a nurse who couldn't see. Others said I couldn't be a psychologist either. "You can't read non-verbal expressions. It's nice you want to help, but why don't you just volunteer?"

The thing was, I didn't want to just volunteer. I wanted to be a productive member of society. I wanted to give back. I got a Guide Dog, went to college and thought I'd prove everyone wrong. This is my big day, I thought.

I rehearsed possible interview questions and my responses. If the interviewer asked why I wanted to work there, I'd extol the values of the hospital, how their attention to health care and detail was legendary and how I enjoyed working in a stimulating environment where this attention was applied. If they asked how I could do my job, I'd share all of the skills I'd practiced.

My mind wandered to the first day of doctoral school when the professor said "None of you will receive special treatment. I will not discriminate, nor will I baby you. If any of you need help, I will provide it. But I will not hold your hand. I tell you this, not because I expect you to expect me to baby you, but so you all know that each and every person here deserves to be here and I will treat you that way. I do not want to hear any comments about affirmative action or special treatment. Those things do not and cannot exist here. I will hold you to high standards and expect you to achieve them. But my door is always open."

She did hold us to incredibly high standards, but her door was always open. She forced us to work on body language and reading expressions. I knew I couldn't do that. With a trembling hand, I knocked on her open door. "Maria, come in. There is a chair to your left." I found the plush leather seat and sat down. "How can I help you?"

"I'm concerned about this body language work. I don't know how I can complete this successfully. I was hoping you might be able to offer some suggestions."

"Well, as you know, I won't exempt you from this assignment."

"Of course. I'll have to deal with these things as a psychologist too."

"Right. So how do you plan to handle this then?"

"I'm not sure. For a lot of this I'm probably going to have to rely on sound."

"What do you mean?"

"Well, I can tell by voices how someone is feeling. I can tell you're interested and not distracted."

"You're right. But you've also had several hours of hearing my voice. How do you know you can tell this with a client who you just met?"

"Doesn't body language vary?"

"Sure, but there are some constants."

"Yeah, there are with voice too. And you can tell a lot about words people use, too."

"Okay, give me examples."

"Okay, someone who's upset or nervous might talk more quickly. If they're using words like hate, hurt, or ticked that's a clue that they're upset too. If they're talking slowly, they could be sad, or struggling."

"Great. That's how I want you to handle this. I don't care if you use the body language. I do want you to learn it, though. That way, if you're in a counseling session and someone is describing the body language of someone else, you can at least attempt to relate."

I snapped back to the present and thought again about the interview. I would tell them about using a tape recorder and journaling after each session. I would tell them how I could use my note taker and laptop to keep accurate records. I could show them how Coco and I work and explain her therapeutic value. If they still seemed hesitant, I'd explain how the fact that I cannot see can be an asset when dealing with people who have body image difficulties.

Finally, the plane landed. The more helpful flight attendant told me I'd have to wait until everyone else had deplaned and they'd help me. "Ma'am, could I please have you let me go? I can find the luggage carousel. I have a job interview to prepare for."

"Sure, are you sure you don't want assistance? I can arrange something."

"If you can do it so I can get off quickly."

"Of course."

"Thank you!"

"No problem. Good luck on that interview."

Luckily, the walk through the airport was much less eventful this time. The person assisting me actually asked me if I'd like to use the rest room. I took that opportunity to prepare myself physically for the interview. I put on my lipstick and eye shadow.

I took a cab to the hospital and found the elevators up to the tenth floor. I had not told them I am blind, so I expected them to be surprised, but I did not expect to be treated the way I was.

"Are you a patient?"

"No, I'm here for an interview."

"Oh, I see... What position?"

"General Psychologist. I'm Maria Michella."

"I'll be back." I heard the man leave, then the sound of frantic, quiet voices behind a closed door.

A woman's hurried footsteps made an intense crescendo as her high-heels came closer to me.

"Miss Michella... Please come with me." I was surprised not to be given a hand to shake, but I obliged anyway. Maybe she was waiting until we were in her office. "You didn't tell us about your condition. We're sorry. We've filled the position. Such a shame you've come all this way. Please, accept my apologies. I'll show you to the door." She grabbed my arm firmly and dragged me toward the door.

After she slammed it, I stood outside the door, trying to collect my thoughts. Why couldn't they have called? Why didn't they interview me anyway, at least giving me a chance to show what I could do? She didn't even introduce herself! That would have been nice! I don't understand. Someone hurried past me, entering the office I'd just left. "I'm Cathy Smith. I'm here for an interview."

"Cathy, come in! You're the first interview we've had for the General Psychologist position. I'm pleased you've come." I told Coco to find outside, choking back tears.

I went to dinner with friends, but I hardly tasted the lobster or heard the conversation. Even though the menu was in Braille and my friends treated me like a normal person, I couldn't shake the sad feeling of inadequacy.

In the time since I'd left Florence's cab, I'd encountered so much prejudice and paternalism. So many people seemed to be out to get me.

I checked into a hotel room and decided to read my email. My spirit soared when I saw an email that looked promising:

From: Judy Clark employment@empoweredpeople.org

To: maria.m@earthlink.net

Subject: An exciting opportunity!

Dear Ms. Michella:

I am excited to tell you that after much consideration, we have decided to offer you the chance to possibly receive employment at our Portland campus. Your credentials are impressive and we look forward to working with you.

However, we are concerned about having a blind psychologist. We are unsure of your ability to carry out many of the tasks a counselor might complete.

Your professor from college has assured us you would fit the bill nicely. However, we would propose a few trial options:

Option One: You could work with one of our supervisors, putting in extra time where we could test your abilities.

Option Two: You could volunteer with us for six months so we can ensure this match will work.

Please get back to me at your earliest convenience!

Sincerely,

Judy Clark

Human Resources Manager

212-234-4321 (Phone)

Come see what empowerment really is! Work with one of our counselors to see the new, empowered, respected you!

A New Lease on Access

For a while now, I've considered myself an advocate. Sometimes, all I can advocate for are my needs as a blind person, but I usually try to consider the needs of others when I advocate. For example, I need Braille signs, but people who use wheelchairs have other needs. If someone wants to know how accessible their space is, I do my best to represent both needs. But until now, I didn't really know any of this from experience. Sure, I have good friends who use wheelchairs, but I never saw what they did or how they navigated situations. But now that I'm not allowed to put any weight on my foot, I'm learning a whole lot about accessibility and getting a whole new perspective on the world. So I'll probably be writing about some of these things in the next little while as I experience them.

Today's Shopping Trip
I needed to refill my pain pill prescription, and the usual pharmacy isn't open right now because of

Memorial Day. So we went to a Super Target to refill the prescription, get some shorts now that I've gained 35 pounds since last summer and grab some coffee on the way out. First we wheeled over to the pharmacy and had to fill out the form because I'm a new customer. I won't go into the form thing because we've already been there before. I will note two accessibility things that may be helpful. First, you can choose whether you want a childproof cap. For someone with limited strength or dexterity, this is a nice thing, although since I've got the bottle, I can tell you that as childproof bottles go, this one is easy to open. The next option is a colored band round the lid. You get to choose the color (I chose blue). The idea is for families to be able to tell their medications apart. I'd imagine this would, in addition to limiting family members' chances of taking the wrong medication, allow people with limited (but somewhat usable) vision to know which medication is theirs. It would be cool, for people who live alone, to be able to have a different color for each medication. I don't know anyone who uses the talking prescription bottle-holders, but these bottles wouldn't work. They're like a triangular pyramid with the lid at the base of the triangle.

    Okay, on to clothes shopping. The aisles are, fortunately, wide enough for a wheelchair, and most of the clothing is within my reach as far as height goes. But let's go into the dressing room. There's a sign for "women" with a wheelchair (the universal symbol for access in the United States). We were given our number and headed into the dressing room. It was a little tricky to get into the room, but then we did finally get there. The first observation I have is that just because a room is large enough to accommodate a wheelchair doesn't mean it's very usable. I haven't figured out how to get my pants on without standing on one foot. Unless I can lean back far enough, I can't get the pants all the way on. If I've got a bed, it's no problem however. But there were no grab bars to help me get from the wheelchair to the little hard bench they provided. Nor were there bars to use to keep my balance. Maybe a more experienced wheelchair user who uses one in normal daily life could've handled this better, but it made shopping very tricky and tiring.

Now on to the clothes themselves. Since I had to stand on one foot and my balance is awful, I have to use a hand on something (sink, bar, wall, whatever). So I'm essentially one-handed while putting clothing on. What is the American obsession with multiple buttons and hooks? How does someone with only one hand access these?

Now that we've got new clothes and picked up our prescription, let's head to the Starbucks inside the Super Target. That's not a big problem, but with all the displays and cases, it's tricky to get to the case. Luckily, Mom was paying, but whenever I go somewhere where you order at a counter, I feel strangely detached from the person. It's even harder to tell if anyone's there and ready to take my order. In a wheelchair, I notice that even fewer people address me. It's so much easier for them to address my Mom I guess. But it makes me wonder, do they do this to people who are sighted and in wheelchairs with this frequency?

Oh, and we still have to get out of the store. Wow, that wheelchair ramp feels steep when you're sitting in the chair. I've always hated how flat some of those are, but I guess I never realized that they're so steep when you're in the chair. It's a good thing I got that latte; I need it after such a tiring day!

Transitioning To College: Ways To Make Sure You Grow And Enjoy!

As some of you will remember, I kind of freaked out about going to college last year. I was so nervous, scared and concerned about how well I would do. Luckily, I have learned a few things about making that transition. I want to share them with you. Whether you're blind or not, have chronic pain or illness or not or just bored, I hope these suggestions will make your transition easier.

Know your resources: Build a tool box
One of the concepts that could have helped me the most if I'd been less hardheaded is having a toolbox. There are several people who have suggested this to me, some who are good friends, others whom I don't know but who know a lot about pain management.

This concept stretches further than managing pain. Knowing your resources is extremely important. Do you have a healer?

If you deal with any chronic conditions, know who you should talk to about any flares. I can't stress the importance of staying in communication with your doctors enough.

Know a list of people who can help you deal with the challenges of college. If you're visually impaired, know where you can get accessible information for college. Decide how you will find out about information posted in residence halls and student centers. Consider asking an R.A. or friend for assistance. Learn who coordinates activities for your dorm and ask that she/he email you or call you when new information is posted about activities, maintenance, changes in rules or regulations or anything else that is posted. Learn where new information will be posted on your college's website. Does your college have a "Daily Update"? If so, read every word.

I'll keep coming back to the toolbox concept as we go through the other challenges.

Manage your stress and schedule

Stress can be one of your worst enemies. For me, too much stress causes an RSD/CRPS flare and headaches that make me sensitive to light, sound and smell. Recognizing the stress levels before they go out of proportion is vital. Recognizing the patterns of stress can be tricky though. You'll be adding a lot of stress trying to learn a new area (sighted, blind or other), eating strange food, meeting new people and trying to live in a smaller space. Build in time specifically for relaxation. Even if, like me, you can't schedule your day and when you'll do it, make sure that each day you take stock of your emotions, physical sensations and spiritual habits. If you're sad, angry or frustrated, figure out why and try to think of at least one small step to get through that emotion. If you're feeling ill or have increased pain, try to figure out why. Decide if you'll need the help of a physician. If you're unsure, call the doctor and ask. Most doctors will help you decide when to come in. If you're feeling spiritual tensions, pray, sing or do whatever you need to do to focus on God.

When you've figured out what areas need help, spend some time in "self-care" mode. Find ways to manage your stress, pain and tension. This is where your toolbox comes in. Take out the relaxation skills, objects to help you deal with the tension and the skills you already have to deal with challenges.

Back when I was on the evil Neurontin not so jokingly referred to as the "pills from hell", I had a very, very hard time dealing with stress. I don't cry much, but I was crying up to three times a week (usually hard for my under-developed tear ducts to handle.) I really couldn't figure out where my toolbox was, not to mention how to use the tools I had. I asked the prayer group I'm in to pray for me (which they have done faithfully). Then, I asked for help. I went down to our Disability Services office and talked to one of the wonderful women who work there. She let me vent and helped me figure out how to manage the stress. When I left, I had a plan of action. Remembering just one skill or tool can make a world of difference!

Asking for Help Makes You More Independent

That sentence looks weird at first glance. For some reason, I always thought of independence as doing absolutely everything on my own. But that's not true. Asking for help politely and appropriately makes you more independent and helps you grow. Sure, I could treat my RSD completely on my own, or, I could ask for help from the doctors and learn how to treat it appropriately. I don't know anyone who would tell me that to be independent, I needed to give myself a sympathetic block. That would be extremely dangerous and could probably cause paralysis. But we often forget that trying to be a hero can cause emotional or spiritual paralysis.

In the example above, I didn't know which way was up. I was mentally paralyzed. Asking for help in that instance helped me function. We need others. We need our faith and we need our tools. Asking for help does not make you weak; it makes you smart for appropriately using your resources and toolbox.

Take It Slow

Last year, when I signed up for only 13 credits for my first semester and then had to drop down to 12, I felt very guilty. Even this summer, I felt guilty for signing up for only 13 credits for this fall. But the more I've learned to read my body, emotions and spirit, I've learned that it is necessary to pace yourself. Taking a full semester while I'm still dealing with pain and recovering from surgery would not be a good idea. Last semester, when I took 16 credits, I pushed myself into a huge flare of RSD. My doctor strongly suggested that I drop a course, but since, at that point, I only had one month, I decided to keep them all. I didn't listen to my body. Pacing myself would have helped me avoid some of the pain. In the end, you have to answer to yourself and to God. I really don't think that in the end, we'll say "darn, I wish I'd taken 4 classes and made myself sick/crazy/completely overwhelmed".

Putting it all together

Your transition can go smoothly. You can enjoy your first year. Most of this advice will help you whether you're transitioning or returning for another year. Pace yourself, ask for help, use your tools and manage your stress. Things won't be perfect, you'll make mistakes, but you will be much better able to handle the challenges.

Relaxation

I was asked if I'd post about the relaxation exercises I've mentioned here. These are based on some of the more common exercises I've found, but modified to suit my purposes. I had to work with the way my mind works and the way my foot acts.

Premise

The premise behind these exercises, for me, has been the idea that my body was designed by God. By doing relaxation exercises, I'm just helping my body to behave as God designed it to. This means that I tend to put God in the center of these activities. The other premise is that the exercise is not as important as the effect. If the exercise makes me feel ill or makes me more tense, I'm not going to keep doing it.

Exercise #1: Prayer

Prayer is an invaluable tool in staying calm and fighting off stress. Often, I need to decompress, but no one is around to do that with. My best tool is prayer. It helps me focus on God, not the circumstances. I like to memorize scripture because it helps to have a ready defense when the negative thoughts come.

Exercise #2: Blogging

Blogging gives me a lot of comfort. Thinking about what I can write about today helps me not think about stress or pain. In thinking about these exercises, for example, I'm not thinking about the pain or stress. This is a healthy way to find out about yourself and your thoughts.

Exercise #3: Breathe

One of the hallmarks of relaxation is deep breathing. I've heard multiple ways to do this, so I don't think there's any wrong or right way. The goal is just to breathe from your stomach or diaphragm. This gets more air into your lungs. Do this as slowly as you can; remember, the goal is to relax, not pass out.

Exercise #4: Imagery

Imagery is a good way to take your mind off your troubles. Here, you want to find an image that works on whatever goal you have for yourself.

If your goal is stress management, find an image that relaxes you (a pond, a peaceful meadow or a stream, for example). If pain management is your goal, try to find an image that represents your pain getting better.

What does your pain or stress feel, smell, look, sound and taste like? What would make those sensations go away? One image I use is a dragon's flame being put out. Another, which represents the nerves behaving themselves is to imagine a healing light traveling from my head down my spine and through my left leg. This is the most successful for me.

Remember that you won't always agree with or like everyone else's image. Your image is uniquely yours, so don't try to change it just because it isn't like mine.

Exercise #5: Relaxing your muscles

This exercise is based somewhat on imagery. Imagine each muscle group getting more relaxed. Some people prefer to use a technique called progressive muscle relaxation. Here, you tense each muscle group, then relax it. I can't do this comfortably, so I don't like it, but you may find it helpful.

Exercise #6: Aesthetic Appreciation

In this exercise, distraction is key. Find an object, food or place that makes you feel good. Then, think about what in this object makes you feel good. Do you like the smell? The taste? The color? The texture? The sound? Focus on these ideas as though you were trying to describe it to your friend. What would you tell her? You don't have to write it down, but it can be helpful if you enjoy writing.

I do this over at Brewberry's or even on a walk. The sensation of Julio's pull against the harness. The smell of the flowers and the freshly cut grass. The taste of the latté and muffin. All of these things are positives. Focusing on them lifts the mood.

Exercise #7: Listen to music

This one is great if you have chronic pain. Studies say that music can reduce pain and depression linked to it by about 20%. Music is a form of distraction, and it works incredibly well.

Create your own!

These are just a few of the things I've used to deal with my stress and pain. You may find others, such as reading a good book or using nice-smelling lotions or essential oils. Whatever you do, just remember, it's not the exercise that's important. Don't critique your breathing technique or beat yourself up if you do it differently than I say. Just relax!

Freedom from Fear and a Chance to Grow

Please bear with me, I woke up to a really messed up bed, meaning that I don't feel much like I actually slept last night. Ugh! But that's not the point of this entry. I want to write more about a concept which I've skirted around for the last while in several entries. If you're good at reading between lines, this won't be news to you, but for my own sake, I think it's time to write this out bluntly, honestly and publicly.

One of my greatest fears is messing up or making mistakes. This can be a healthy fear because it makes me strive to do my best, but I've let it keep me from doing things I want, and need, to do.

Somewhere in my brain, I decided that messing up was not only bad for me; it was bad for everyone else too. For example, it would be the end of the world if I fumbled with my mobility skills because someone might think that blind people were not able to be self-sufficient or travel safely. If I spilled a glass of water, that action would have a ripple effect down to all other blind people and people would ask us all to use sippy cups. I'm exaggerating slightly, but you get the idea, right?

This concept didn't just stick to blindness; it stuck in other corners of my life. In my writing, I was always afraid to make a mistake in how I talked about a source article or person. When I wrote for the school newspaper, I was afraid that my sources would hate me for getting something wrong. It was even worse for the community newspaper, even though I was only speaking from my personal experience. My articles might give a wrong impression. In this journal, and in my delicious links, I fear summarizing a source wrong, missing the point or using the writing in a way it wasn't intended. Thus, if you look at my delicious links, you'll see several links with notes that say "great article", "beautiful writing", or some other fluff. That's not to say that these aren't great articles, they are. The problem is that my synopsis of "great article" means nothing! How angry would we all be if the next issue of "Braille Book Review" came out with book synopses like that?

This attitude puts a damper on activities or memories of them. I left CSUN, having enjoyed myself thoroughly, but wondering if people thought I was a bumbling idiot. I didn't have any proof of that attitude, in fact, I got to meet a lot of cool people and learn new things. They've even talked to me after the conference, which they wouldn't have to do. In that case, some of my fears were probably warranted. I was so in awe of all of the cool people, experiences and technology, I probably didn't always act like myself. I was also stubborn, hardheaded and dumb about the way I managed the pain (I don't think being told that you have to stop throwing up so you can get on the plane home before it leaves because you're in so much pain shows a good sense of pain management). The point is, that in this case, I spent too much time worrying about all of these issues, instead of relaxing, being myself and having fun. Being afraid to make a mistake probably lead me to make more. And the time I spent after the conference while I was in so much pain was complicated by the extra, unneeded stress.

    This attitude is really harmful. It leads to excess stress, which in turn leads to more pain. When I spend time worrying about making mistakes, I lose a chance to make a difference. What I say, do or write might end up helping someone. Maybe, just maybe, one small action, word or article can change someone's thoughts. It will probably be a small change, but small changes can lead to bigger changes. Small changes can lead to movements. If I'm so focused on myself, worrying about what others think of me or fearing that I will ruin it for EVERYONE, it's egotistical. Instead, I can focus on the moment and make a difference.

This attitude is also spiritually unhealthy. When I focus on me, I'm making myself seem bigger than God. Do I really mean to say that God is smaller than my screw-ups? It puts it in perspective, doesn't it? God knows I'm going to make mistakes. Yes, I should strive to grow, but striving to grow doesn't mean being fearful of making mistakes. I need to let go and let God as they say.

Imagine if I'd been too afraid to attempt going to college. What good would that have done? Sure, I made mistakes last year, but I also got a huge chance to grow. I'm not afraid of living on my own anymore. I've seen God move in my life too many times this year to want to take it back. Or, what if I'd been afraid to go to convention in Vegas on my own? I would have lost the chance to see some very cool people and things. If nothing else, that convention taught me about safety and that I really could trust God and myself.

So, before all of you that made it to the bottom of this, I'm making a pledge to try. I'm going to try to let go and feel free to try. Maybe I'll make mistakes; I might even end up with tears and frustration. But I will not deprive God of the chance to use me, myself of the chance to grow or anyone who wants to watch the chance to learn with me.

Assisting a Guide Dog Team

When thinking about helping a Guide Dog team, it is important to understand how the team travels. A guide dog is trained to walk in a straight line, except when guiding around obstacles. The dog is trained to guide around obstacles, stop for changes in elevation such as curbs and stairs and use intelligent disobedience to protect itself and the blind handler.

Looking for a Good Route

Sometimes, the dog or handler may not travel routes that others would use easily. To find a good route, consider these questions. It might also be helpful to walk the route with the handler before teaching the team together. This gives the handler an opportunity to help decide if the route is appropriate, and understand the route better.

* Are there cues the handler can hear, feel or see, if the handler has low vision, to know when to tell the dog to turn?
* Are there clear landmarks the dog can use as cues to turn, if none are present for the handler?
* Does the route avoid crossing large open spaces like parking lots or patches of grass?
* What possible pitfalls are part of the route? How can they be avoided?
* What non-essential landmarks could help the handler be sure she or he is on the right track?

Seeking a good landmark

What constitutes a good landmark depends on the handler's preferences and abilities. However, good landmarks usually have similar characteristics. If the handler has low vision, it might be helpful to look for landmarks that the handler can see, but keep in mind that vision can sometimes change from day to day and be ineffective at night. Look for landmarks based on sound, touch and even smell. Is there a bakery, an open area that echoes or a big hill that the handler can use as a landmark? Also, remember that street crossings and blocks can be counted as landmarks, but it is helpful to have something else to reassure that the handler is on track.

Dos and Don'ts for Teaching the Team

Do explain the route before setting out.

Do give directions to the handler.

Do walk behind the guide dog team to avoid distracting the dog. Off the right shoulder is best.

Do give advanced warning if a moving turn is required. A moving turn is generally one that comes mid-block or inside a building.

Do tell the handler if the dog has no choice but to turn.

Do allow the handler to practice obedience if the dog loses focus.

Do give guidance about when to make major turns.

Do use sighted guide for patterning challenging routes.

Don't give directions to the dog.

Don't signal the dog to make turns. This may give the handler a false sense of security that they understand the route well.

Don't tell the guide dog team how and when to avoid obstacles. Even if the dog makes a mistake, this can be an important learning experience for the dog and handler.

Don't physically touch or handle the dog or handler, even if you don't think the dog will guide around a specific obstacle. This distracts the team, and can send a confusing message to the dog. Remember, you won't always be there to help the team, so hands off is best.

How the Team Crosses a Street

A guide dog team follows a certain protocol to cross the street safely. This procedure is how Guide Dogs for the Blind recommended crossing the street in 2004. Knowing this will help when choosing and explaining a route and aid you in crossing the street safely with the dog and handler.

When the dog comes to the end of the block, he will bring the handler to the curb, preferably, the curb cut. The handler, feeling that the dog has stopped, probes with a foot and feels that she has reached the end of the block. If crossing at this particular street, she waits to hear that it is safe to cross, then commands the dog "forward". If the handler needs to make a turn at the intersection, she makes the turn ONLY after reaching the curb at the end of the block.

A Few Definitions and Concepts

Here are some terms a guide dog team may use when using guidework.

Obedience: A practiced series of commands such as sit, down and stay that help the handler make sure the dog is focused.

Patterning: Showing a route to the dog multiple times with positive re-enforcement such as food or a toy at key landmarks and destinations. This can be done using the dog to guide, using a cane or using sighted guide. Either of these methods work, but guide dog schools generally recommend using a cane or sighted guide for tricky destinations.

Traffic check: The practice of allowing the dog to avoid traffic if the handler misjudges the situation or when a car acts in an unexpected way.

Intelligent disobedience: The skill used by the dog to avoid obstacles and perform traffic checks if the dog judges the situation unsafe. One common example is refusing to obey the "forward" command if traffic is moving in front of the team.

Surge: The sound of traffic when drivers step on the gas pedal when the light is green. This allows the handler to make a decision about crossing the street.

Distraction: Anything that causes the dog to lose focus. Using the phrase "dog distraction", for example, allows the handler to know why the dog might become distracted.

Sighted Guide: A method of guiding a blind person safely, conveniently and with dignity. Allow the person with a visual impairment to hold onto your arm, just above the elbow. If the person uses a guide dog, offer them the left arm. The person can follow your body movements if you hold your arm naturally, or with a bend at the elbow, but keep your arm close to your body. Stop for changes in elevation such as stairs or curbs. Warn the person when the area is too narrow for the two of you to pass through it safely by moving your arm behind you, as if reaching into your back pocket. Warn of overhanging obstacles, and allow the person to protect himself or herself.

Further Assistance

The handler should always be the first contact when questions arise relating to the safety or ability of a guide dog team. If the handler is unsure, or you feel the situation is unsafe and cannot be resolved without further assistance, allow the handler to call the guide dog school where the team was trained.

Acknowledgements

Many "Nickie's Nook" readers contributed valuable feedback and suggestions for drafts of this information. Thanks also go to Guide Dogs for the Blind, where Nickie and Julio were trained.

For more information about Guide Dogs for The Blind, visit www.guidedogs.com or call 1-800-295-4050.

The Philosophy of Guide Dog Public Relations

At the age of sixteen, I made the decision to apply to receive and train with a guide dog. I hoped my mobility and ease of travel would increase as I learned to work with my dog. I did not predict some of the public relations challenges I would face as my dog, Julio, and I worked as a team to navigate safely. I daily come up against claims, both true and false, that others believe about guide dogs. People believe that my dog reads traffic lights. They also believe that my dog knows where I want to go, and understands commands like "take me to the mall". They claim it is important to yield for a guide dog team when in traffic, and that other dogs can distract him. We can examine these claims philosophically to determine their veracity.

The philosopher, Socrates, developed a method of taking apart claims and proving them either true or false. This method is called an elenchus. An elenchus examines claims for contradictions that prove they cannot be true. We perform elenchuses every day without being aware that we are performing them. For example, to perform an elenchus on the claim that guide dogs read traffic lights, one must first examine the statement and determine what is necessary for this statement to be true. For a dog to read traffic lights, it is necessary for the dog to be able to see the traffic light, and for the dog to be able to comprehend the meaning of colors. Since a guide dog usually stands between twenty and twenty-eight inches at the shoulder, and a traffic light is between ten and twenty feet tall, it would be impossible for the dog to see the traffic light. In addition, scientists have determined that dogs cannot see color, but instead see shades of grey; it would be impossible for a dog to interpret the color and meaning of a traffic light. Thus, it is impossible for a dog to read a traffic light. In this case, the contradictions are that the dog must be able to see the light, but cannot, and that the dog must comprehend colors but do not.

    We have resolved that the claim that guide dogs read traffic lights is false by the use of reason, but it would also be possible to determine this another way. One could, in theory observe a guide dog team as they cross the street. To be scientifically accurate, one could observe many teams and notice how they cross the street. If one were to observe a team, that person would notice the following pattern. The team would walk up to the curb at a crosswalk and stop. The handler might adjust her alignment, or just simply stand still. When the light turns green for the team to cross, the observer and handler would hear a surge of traffic. The handler would tell his dog "forward" and the team would walk across the street. This pattern would develop each time a team crossed at an intersection with a traffic light. Even if the observer did not notice the sound of the surge in traffic as drivers for the parallel traffic began moving, he would still notice that the team began moving only at the handler's command. Thus, it would be logical to infer that the dog responded to the handler's command, not the change in color of the traffic light. I suspect this claim comes from a misunderstanding of how a guide dog team travels. People are unaware that Julio and I really do work as a team, and that we each have responsibilities to make sure we travel safely and effectively. In addition, since people who are sighted do not need to rely on their ears, they probably do not think about the sound traffic makes when drivers all accelerate at the same time. It seems logical, then, that it would be impossible for a blind person to make the decision of when to cross the street. In this case, a lack of information leads people to a false claim.

To examine the claim that guide dogs understand locations and destinations as commands, both reason and observation demonstrate the falsehood of the claim. While dogs may understand more than humans give them credit for, they do not understand long, drawn-out commands. A guide dog handler or instructor will tell anyone who asks that dogs can understand concepts, such as right and left, but word associations, such as chair, door and outside are sometimes more difficult because the meaning of these words can change. A chair, for example, can be anything from a La-Z-Boy to a park bench. Word associations generally need to be used in an area near where the sought-after object is located. This means that it would be unfair to expect a guide dog to understand locations such as mall, restaurant and store. If I observe a guide dog team, I see that the handler actually gives directions such as "right" and "left", not "Take me to the mall." This belief probably comes from false depictions of guide dog teams in print and on television.

Next, I can prove that it is important to yield to a guide dog team when the team is crossing a street by the use of reason. Obviously, if a car, which moves faster and is larger than a pedestrian hits the pedestrian, it will injure that pedestrian. Moreover, while a guide dog helps keep its blind handler safe by watching for, listening for and avoiding traffic, a car can move more quickly than a dog. Finally, because of these dangers, no one argues that a car should not yield for a sighted pedestrian. Therefore, if we believe we are responsible for helping keep others safe, then, for the reasons above, it is important to yield for a guide dog team, and this claim is true. Since serious harm could come to a guide dog team if we conducted an observation of what happens if drivers do not yield, it would be unethical to conduct that observation. This belief probably comes from campaigns surrounding pedestrian safety, and an increased education effort to teach drivers about the need to yield for all pedestrians, especially those who are blind.

Finally, it is possible to prove that other dogs can distract guide dogs through reason and observation. Distraction means that the guide dog is focusing, at least in part, on something other than guiding its handler. So, if we can be reasonably certain that another dog's appearance is interesting to a guide dog, and that this interest takes the dog's attention away from guiding, then it follows that the dog's response may be a cause of the distraction. If I observe what happens when a guide dog sees a dog, I might see that when the guide dog notices the dog, the guide tries to go play with the other dog. I might also notice the handler working to refocus the dog's attention by asking the guide to perform tasks like "sit" and "down". However, I have not actually observed a cause. Therefore, in this case, we cannot observe a cause and effect, but we can infer that the other dog distracts the guide dog. The belief that guide dogs can be distracted probably arises from observations like the one I have outlined.

    The ways in which I examined these claims to determine their veracity are not new. Two philosophers, Renae Descartes and David Hume both examined claims to determine if they were true. Descartes used reason to determine veracity. When he started his famous meditations, he stated "...I don't need to show each of my beliefs to be false. I may never be able to do that, but since reason now convinces me that I ought to withhold my ascent just as carefully from what isn't obviously certain and indubitable as from what's obviously false, I can justify the rejection of all my beliefs if in each I can find some ground for doubt." (Kessler, 262). Descartes' method takes each claim apart into the smallest parts it is formed from, decides what parts of the claim should be doubted and thrown out, builds up his claim with the indubitable pieces of the claim and publishes his work for others to read and critique. By this method, Descartes believed he could find certitude.

David Hume, on the other hand, believed reason can only get us so far. He chose to use his senses to record careful observations. The observer, he believed, should avoid drawing conclusions as she or he observed. The observation should only contain what the observer actually sensed. For example, in his writing "An Enquiry Concerning Human Understanding", Hume states "Adam, though his rational faculties be supposed, at the very first entirely perfect, could not have inferred from the fluidity and transparency of water that it would suffocate him..." (Hume, 274). Hume then explains that we can only observe a series of actions, not a cause and effect. This is why we could only observe a dog, and a guide dog's actions after seeing the dog, but not an actual cause and effect. Instead, we could infer the cause. Hume also explains that we cannot be certain that our observations will be true in the future. He claims that we cannot be certain that the sun will rise tomorrow, because we cannot observe that action ahead of time.

In summary, we have examined four claims about guide dogs, and proven two to be true and two to be false. We have discovered that both Descartes and Hume have methods of determining truth that work equally well in this area. Both reason and observation can help us better understand how a guide dog team works together.

Works Cited

Descartes, Renae. "Meditation I." Voices of Wisdom. Ed. Gary E. Kessler. Boston: Thomson-Wadsworth, 2007. 263-269.

Hume, David. "An Enquiry Concerning Human Understanding." Voices of Wisdom. Ed. Gary E. Kessler. Boston: Thomson-Wadsworth, 2007. 271-277.

The Intersection of Pain and Blindness

As a little girl, I began to notice that when I heard the words "because you're blind", it usually meant one of two things. Either I was about to be excluded from doing something with my peers, or I was about to be told I had to work harder. I also learned that if I complained, it wouldn't change facts. Somewhere along the line, I got the impression it isn't okay to acknowledge my differences. Blindness isn't an excuse became a mantra. That doesn't mean I became super independent, or even extremely successful. It means I carry a lot of guilt. I've only recently started acknowledging that sometimes, doing something differently is no fun, and more importantly, it's okay to feel annoyed or angry at injustices I see. Acknowledging this does not make me weak or a disgrace.

As I've spent time thinking about how to help myself deal with the pain, I've noticed that blindness makes a difference in how I approach my pain, and it is important to acknowledge these differences and be honest about them with myself and doctors. Too many times, I found myself unwilling to admit that things are different for me, and accept help when I need it. As I've conversed with others about this new revelation, I started to realize I can't be the only one dealing with this. If there are as many people with vision problems as the powers that be claim there are, and if the statistic of one in five people being in pain holds true in the blind community, then this issue has to be more prevalent than we usually acknowledge it to be. So, I decided to do something about it. My short-term goal, to be accomplished with this writing or more if necessary, is to get a conversation started. I'm just going to use my own narrative, since I have permission to do this, and make some conjectures and "what if" statements. I hope that this won't just be a sob story, but instead a conversation starter both between people who are blind and between patients and doctors, help others discover the ways medical conditions and blindness intersect and give hope to others. To do this, I'm going to tease out some common themes and perspectives and examine them from the aspect of blindness as a part of the whole person who comes to be treated for chronic pain. I'll use the biopsychosocialspiritual model of looking at the whole person to examine these ideas.

Biological and Physical

One of the first aspects usually discussed in regards to pain of any kind is the biological or physical cause. Scientists have discovered substances and neurotransmitters that cause and increase pain. They've shown that pain can cause depression, and, conversely, people who have depression feel more pain. Sleep problems often arise from chronic pain, and make the perception of pain worse. The obvious questions, does blindness increase the likelihood of either of these two issues? I can't answer the question about depression; I don't even know if there is a connection. But I do know that there are several studies right now related to blindness and sleep problems. It seems likely that between pain and blindness, sleep problems could be made worse, or even be more likely to occur, although I have no data to back up this claim. As for depression, while I have not seen literature on this, I do know that darkness can increase some depression's effects. Seasonal Affective Disorder may be a good example of this. I'm not saying that blindness causes depression, but asking if it has an effect on this aspect of pain.

The next important aspect of pain is its cause. Even if there is no cure for the cause of the pain, doctors want to know why the pain is caused to best treat it, and patients need a name for their pain and, possibly, something to research to become better informed and seek out needed resources and support. This may or may not be impacted by blindness. I know, in my case, blindness complicates the question of "what color is it?" I sometimes get the answer "I've seen it worse." And this is supposed to be comforting? Also, what color is that? I should explain that my condition, Reflex Sympathetic Dystrophy or Complex Regional Pain Syndrome can cause a lot of strange things such as changes in the color of the limb that's affected. If I go to the pain clinic, I can't tell them it's the color of "I've seen it worse", can I? And what about blind people who live on their own (which I plan to do)? How do they answer this question? I don't blame the doctors on this one. I know that a blue foot, or a purple hand is not good, and probably played an important role in my diagnosis with RSD. I'm not sure what the best solution is to this question. This is where I play assertive person and ask the question "well, what color is THAT supposed to mean?" It usually works. But this may be a barrier for me being able to gauge when I need to go to the doctor or not... But I'm getting ahead of myself. Another question to be asked in the case of finding the cause is whether some accommodation the blind patient makes could cause the pain. For example, if I constantly miss curbs, and twist my ankle; that could play an important role in knowing what to look for. In my case, I couldn't tell the doctors for sure how or why the pain started the first time. It wasn't like the second injury, where I felt my ankle give and had that sinking feeling of knowing I'd screwed up big time. I'm assuming this complicated my doctors' job somewhat.

Now we need to examine the self-care needs of a patient who is blind. In my opinion, one of the biggest needs I have as someone with pain is the ability to use self-determination. I need to be able to get information I need and then, judging from experience or on the basis of that information, make the best decision I can at the time. This poses several dilemmas. [First, the information aspect. For me to get information, I have to have some basic information. So if there is some information like the color of my foot that a doctor needs to give a diagnosis or suggestion for treatment, I need to get that information. If I'm looking for information on self-care, I need to know as much about my diagnosis, treatment and symptoms to watch for as possible.

Finally, my doctor needs to be aware of barriers to my treatment.

To gain information, it is my responsibility to use sighted assistance as I would use a reader or screen reading program. I need to figure out what to look for, and ask the right questions. Sometimes, I have a guide that tells me what to look for, so I know what to ask. With a reader, I might have a worksheet, thesis statement or research question. I can then use that information to ask questions that the reader can help me answer. I can ask what the Bible dictionary says about temptation, for example. In medicine, if I know that color and hair and nail growth are important things to be aware of with CRPS, I can ask about those things. But, we don't always get a neat little guide or have enough knowledge to be able to ask critical questions. In this case, the best I can do is ask "Does my foot look weird?" These questions do have benefits, of course. If I constantly focus only on color, I might miss other odd things because I'm limiting my research or question.

Another problem I face when gaining information is relative inaccessibility of health information available to me as a blind person. I can get basic information with some sites like Webmd, but even that information is limited. I still remember the first summer three and a half years ago when I researched information about "foot pain." It was so frustrating to see pages of great information, but realize that they weren't helpful because they asked where the pain was on a diagram of the body, or used a diagram to demonstrate the part of the foot with the specified symptoms. Now that I have the diagnosis of RSD, I realize how poorly a lot of pain-related sites are designed for people who use screen readers. Unlabeled graphics are common, and they make it hard to find the information I seek. And don't even get me started on the lack of accessible books on pain. I could scan them, but the constant up and down of scanning and the need to stand most of that time makes me hesitant. I don't want to dwell on the RSD; I refuse to give this awful disorder any more of a foot-hold (pun not intended), on my life, but I do want to have enough information to live a full and active life. And many books I've seen seem to be good for this, but they are not accessible to me.

The last issue with information I've seen is that very few handouts are accessible to me. Most of my doctors are great about giving me the information I need to make good decisions about life with the medications they prescribe, but I'm forgetful. Information on exercises, medications, treatments or coping strategies can be overwhelming. And I'm hesitant to involve yet another person in my care. Having a nurse give the information to both me and my family is a good idea in theory, but becomes problematic when you realize that I don't live with them during the school year. And questions arise at awkward times of day. Asking random dorm mates to read this information is something I'm not comfortable with. It gets so frustrating dealing with this pain; I don't want to make it larger than it already is. And, let's face it, not everyone likes reading medical information.

    Then, of course, comes the difficulty in figuring out treatments and whether they work. First, there is the issue of barriers to treatment. If I were a heavy drinker, or drug user, my doctor would need to know that. If I'm dealing with pain-related depression, my doctor needs to know this, too. Also, blindness poses some interesting barriers itself. I'm not comfortable sharing my health information with other people in the lobby, however, and I wouldn't want to share some of that information with my parents if it were true.

    I am fortunate to have great working relationships with all of the doctors I see now. My doctors do not rely on questionnaires to find out about drugs and depression. I know that the pain clinic uses them, but they are not the only or even dominant method of discussing these issues. My doctors are great about being trustworthy, and I can be completely honest with them. The questions get asked and answered honestly, and there has never been a time where I have felt like I was not trusted. This, in my opinion, is how things should be. I also know that I can admit that I am frustrated, though it is incredibly hard for me to do, no matter who I'm talking to. So, for me, giving appropriate information is not a problem anymore.

Finally, I have pain issues that are specific to blindness. This is where that whole part about not wanting to admit things really comes into play. For example, when I had my surgery last May, my doctor encouraged me to stay over night in the hospital. Her reasoning was that I would not feel like learning to use crutches right after surgery. In the hospital, my pain could be managed if the RSD decided it was time to be a brat, and I could learn crutches in the morning. She said she thought crutches might be more challenging for a blind person. Honestly, I wanted to prove people wrong. But I was also scared of the pain issues. If something was going to happen, I was going to make sure it happened at the hospital. That turned out to be one of the smartest decisions, since the nausea was awful and

I needed an IV, medication and lots of buckets. I'm sure someone is going to say that my blindness shouldn't have had anything to do with it. For me, though, it did. Because I stayed, we were able to find out that a walker was safer for me than crutches. That's not giving into blindness, that's being smart. In this case, the definition of independence was admitting I needed help and accepting it as gracefully as one can after surgery. I told that story to show that there are very good reasons to recognize these barriers, so we can effectively address them and hopefully improve quality of life, safety and comfort.

    Let's look at some of these barriers. Most, but not all, of the barriers here are from my own experience. The first barrier I've had to acknowledge is that doctors just don't know what it's like to be blind. How can they help me address pain in a way that's safe for Julio and me if they don't understand our partnership and how we work? If the guide dog school says one thing and I hear the other from my doctors, how do I recognize both perspectives and integrate them? For example, I've heard the comment from people that I walk fast with Julio. People wonder how we can walk so fast if I'm in so much pain. What they don't know is that I'm supposedly a slow walker compared to other handlers. This posed an interesting question, is it safe or beneficial to have a guide dog? I resolved the question by examining how I traveled before I got Julio, and how I travel now. Walking with a guide dog increases my independence and safety. I find walking next to Julio means I have better balance and less stress. This is important because I am more efficient traveling, and able to accomplish more. My stamina is increased. But I still have to accommodate the increase in speed. This also means that doctors and therapists can't judge pain levels by walking speed as easily with me. There was also the added concern about having surgery once I had Julio. I put it off for about two years. I know it added stress for doctors trying to help me. Having RSD is bad enough, but dealing with that and my unwillingness to have surgery was probably very difficult. Now that we may have to consider more drastic options, we have the added concern of messing with any sensory perception. I'm hesitant to consider options like a spinal cord stimulator, since I fear the tingling would mess up my sense of feeling in my foot. I'm fortunate that my doctors are willing to consider these options differently because they treat each patient separately. In other words, they treat me like Nickie, not patient 343 with the bad foot. Some basic considerations for people who are blind and deal with chronic pain include working with a guide dog, staying oriented and managing medications to make this possible, balance issues, identifying medications, getting appropriate directions and other questions and issues too numerous for me to write them down here.

Psychological

The next aspect of pain that must be addressed is the psychological aspect. Many chronic pain sites suggest that chronic pain can be aggravated by underlying psychological challenges such as depression. Similarly, depression is frequently caused by chronic pain. These issues can pose challenges for the person who is blind and has chronic pain that a sighted person might not face, or may face to a lesser extent. Daily life challenges increase stress, advice given about blindness cannot always be applied to dealing with pain and blindness community dynamics can increase stress and, for some people, may increase feelings of guilt and frustration. Each of these psychological challenges can be dealt with, but they must be discussed and acknowledged openly. The voices of people with pain must be heard in the blindness community to make changes and encourage a healthy psychological response to pain.

Stress can increase the perception of pain. Since stress is a fight or flight response, it makes sense that our bodies might respond to pain to a greater extent when we are experiencing stress. With RSD/CRPS, the heightened use of the sympathetic nervous system can increase the pain experience and cause a flare. A blind person can accomplish anything a sighted person can, but people who are blind must sometimes use more skills and experience more stress than the average sighted person. For example, travel requires more planning and more attention to detail for me. On a short bus and light rail trip, I need to engage in more planning and accept more help than my fellow passengers. Using the bus requires that I either call the bus company or use their on-line trip planner to get the information about which buses to take and when. If the route is unfamiliar to me, I am required to call and get as many details as possible about the route. It's not enough to know I need bus 80 on the corner of Smith and Granny; I must know where the bus stops. I need to know that it's the northwest corner of the intersection on Granny and the bus is going south. If possible, I need to know where on the block the bus will stop and if there are any landmarks. If I'm not at the stop exactly, I may be passed by the bus. Light rail requires a lot of trust in my dog, or cane skills. Since I can't read the signs to know where the train will stop and which one it will be, I must seek some form of sighted assistance. Crossing the street at a light rail station is challenging because I am not always sure which way to go to get to the appropriate crosswalk. In short, anything a sighted person takes for granted that they will have access to may be unavailable in its current form. This doesn't mean that I can't travel, only that travel is more stressful. Many tasks are like this; it isn't just travel. This doesn't have to limit me; I'm not proposing that we not engage in these tasks, just that we start acknowledging that tasks can be more stressful and start doing things to mitigate that effect on our pain. This may mean having a "survival" plan in place. I always carry enough cash or checking account balance to get a cab home. That way, if enjoying myself on the trip means I'm tired or in too much pain, I don't have to worry about how I'll get home. I used to believe this was cheating, but I now feel it's smart use of resources. It's a better option than never leaving the house. I also try to carry a small snack and a bottle of water with me, though I don't always remember. This way, if I'm overly hungry or thirsty, or need medication, I can travel more comfortably. A sighted person may just look for a restaurant, but I don't have the luxury of reading signs or a GPS unit yet. I can definitely ask people for help "Do you see any restaurants near here?" This works well when I'm feeling good, but when I'm tired, hungry and in pain, it's not the best method. I think there's a rule that says "when you need it, you can't find it." I can run into benches all day, but when I really need to sit down, I won't find one, for example.

Next there is the issue of good intentions and advice that works for blindness but not for pain. First, blindness is difficult to accept if you've been sighted all of your life, but people understand the challenge to accept it. Sighted people are understanding when a blind person asks for help. I've gotten the feeling that it's okay to not like being blind, but not okay to struggle with accepting pain. Blind people, on the other hand, want to encourage independence and acceptance. A "well-adjusted" blind person shouldn't need help, after all. None of my friends have this attitude, but I have definitely been told this before. The advice not to ask for help and do everything anyone else can do is good, but not to the extent of hurting your health. This came into play when I went through orientation and mobility training. My instructor was smart and helped me learn to pace travel, but I always questioned whether I was "a bad blind person" for being unable to travel perfectly.

Finally, the dynamics of the blind community can cause some major psychological challenges. Sometimes, it seems we get into a contest to see who is "the best blind person." I've been ripped to shreds before because people felt my skills weren't good enough. So now, when I do things differently because of the pain, that's one of the first fears I have. It's so easy to jump to conclusions and distance ourselves from people who we feel aren't well-adjusted enough or skilled enough. But when we're in the other seat, it's incredibly painful. I've been told not to mess up because people would think "all blind people are like that". This attitude causes fear, which increases that fight or flight response. This may not be a problem for every blind person, but I extended these feelings of guilt and inadequacy to dealing with my pain. "If I were only a better person," I say "I wouldn't need to do x y and z to deal with my pain." I wouldn't say that to my social work clients when I have them, so why do I say it to myself?

Fortunately, there are solutions to deal with all of the challenges I discussed. First, we need to admit that there is a problem. Admitting that blindness complicates chronic pain is the first step. Then educating others about these challenges will hopefully help give others with pain the chance to express their voice. I believe both consumer organizations and individuals can have a positive role in helping with all aspects of pain management, but only if we start talking about it.

Next, I think relaxation can be built into each person's day, and thus can mitigate some of the stress issues with pain. Relaxation exercises can be different for everyone because what is relaxing to one person can be stress-provoking for another. Studying relaxation information thoroughly can help a person create a program that works for them. If this is too difficult, meeting with someone trained in relaxation might help. I've found that using relaxation techniques helps make my medication work better, and also helps me deal with the nausea that accompanies high pain levels. Learning relaxation techniques to enhance travel and daily life might make travel less stressful. Redefining independence as doing the best that you can with the resources you have will also help.

Social

The next aspect of pain is its social implications. The largest implication, for me, is that unless someone sees my foot turn purple or notices the brace or cane, they won't know I'm in pain. How do I explain that I can't hang out because I've got this disease no one's ever heard of? It's very strange going from people recognizing blindness immediately, to no one knowing what on earth I'm dealing with. I'm so used to trying to prove that I'm "just like everyone else," that I feel awkward saying "I really shouldn't do that."

The next issue with the social aspect of pain is logistics. I'm challenged enough by transportation issues as a blind person, but when I'm also dealing with pain, it's even more challenging. Taking the bus is great, but severely limits me to how far away I can go. If I want to enjoy myself on my social outing, I can't expect to walk seven blocks each way and enjoy the concert. Taking a cab is another option, but it costs money, which college students need to monitor closely. If I know about these two challenges, I'm more likely to just stay home. This could severely limit my social life.

Spiritual

Finally, the spiritual aspect of pain is, in my opinion, poorly understood. When you add in any other aspect, it could be enough to make your head spin. I'm not a theologian, and am uncomfortable trying to write about spirituality on a macro level, so I'll continue to work with my own narrative here. At church, I found that people couldn't always understand why blindness isn't a big deal to me, but pain is. They felt that blindness must be so much worse than pain. I've never felt this way, though, and it makes it harder to discuss the pain and my spiritual struggles with it. I even find myself wondering if I'm a bad Christian for struggling with the issues of "why me?" and the feelings of fear and guilt. People automatically assume that I have the coping skills, when really, sometimes I'm just saying things are fine when I feel like I'm about to fall apart. I can see some people feeling that blindness and pain are too much, or feeling guilty for feeling that way. I often find my thinking "I can deal with blindness, and believe it's a gift from God, but what am I supposed to do with pain?" I believe honest discussions about disability in the church will help clarify this issue. For now, being honest about struggles and seeking knowledge and wisdom is a great place to start.

I set out to write something other than a sob story or train wreck piece, and I will keep my promise. I believe there are ways to deal with the issues I've presented here. The first step, as I've already mentioned, is to be honest about how these two pieces of our lives (pain and blindness) intersect and affect us. We must break the fear and bring these issues out for discussion. It is my belief that the consumer organizations and those not involved in them can both play an integral role in helping people who have pain and people who are blind. We've found ways to advocate for change and offer support in areas as diverse as Braille, education, job-seeking and Guide Dogs. I believe we can take the good energy from those experiences and use it to transform the experience of pain for others who are blind. I'm not sure how this will happen, only that it can.

I've spoken in this article and others about how my experiences dealing with life with blindness and chronic pain. It is my hope that others will use their voice to share their experiences so we can address them further. Maybe there are more common barriers that I haven't shared here. This isn't meant to be the end-all authority, just a starting point. Please use the comments here or the email form to share any thoughts that come to mind. I'd love to start a dialogue about this.

Independence? Interdependence?

Part of the reason I went into a creative slump was my procrastination. I had several pieces I wanted to write and hadn't yet because I didn't feel I could do them justice (I might write on procrastination later.) The other part was that for safety reasons, I didn't want to reveal what I'd been doing. See, my parents went on a mission trip for ten days or so, so I was home alone for much of that time. And while I'm not aware of any creeps reading my blog, I don't think a creep would exactly make himself or herself known.

So, even though I wanted to write about handling things as independently as possible, I didn't do it. Now, though, Mom and Dad are back, so I feel safe writing about this experience.

I didn't really think I'd gained enough skills after a year away to succeed in the home environment. For one thing, our home is very different from a dorm. It's quieter, for one, and there aren't people living less than ten feet away to ask for visual help. Add to that that there's no cafeteria where I can get dinner prepared and I was afraid. But I didn't want to have a babysitter, and I couldn't go to some of the normal places I'd go since it's a challenge to get up and down stairs. So, we arranged for someone to hang out at our place for a few nights, I went to friends' for two other nights and the rest was me on my own. Since it's still challenging to walk with Julio (balancing a walker and dog is challenging), and we have stairs covered by a ramp that helps, but is challenging to navigate safely with a walker, dog and visual impairment, we got yet another friend to come relieve Julio. Mom and I bought frozen meals for when I was home alone, and I learned to use a microwave and toaster from a wheelchair in a pretty inaccessible kitchen.

I, of course, knew who to call if I needed any help, and thankfully, just checking in with the friend who relieved Julio when she came was sufficient to answer questions I might have. Surprisingly to me, it wasn't that bad. The worst was trying to navigate with the walker or wheelchair, but I think I learned a lot about spatial orientation.

Mom helped me by labeling meals and writing directions for the meals so that I could cook them without guessing. This worked well, and I'm proud to say that I never went hungry. I got good at organizing myself, and didn't have any health crises. The worst thing that happened was a small burn when the inside of my forearm came into contact with the toaster.

This confirmed several things to me. First, at the end of the day, it doesn't matter how perfectly or horribly you complete a task, as long as you complete it to the best of your ability and you find a way to complete it ethically. It didn't matter that I used frozen meals and leftovers to feed myself, nor did it matter that I had to practice backing up and re-entering just to get into the kitchen. In the end, I ate well enough to make it through the day without getting more hungry than normal and I still got into the kitchen. I also had it reinforced to me that it is okay to ask for help. Having help to relieve Julio was not the end of the world. If I'd tried to prove that I could do it, it would have been foolish, dangerous and possibly resulted in a trip to the emergency room.

This isn't to say that I didn't get frustrated or experience cabin fever. Given the choice, I would have preferred spending the week on both feet and in a house or apartment in a city with a bus line near by. And I wish I were a better cook. But truthfully, everyone experiences these frustrations. Not all college students can cook wonderfully. People who can see sometimes don't have all of the tools they'd like to have at their disposal. Most importantly, everyone needs help. It was most important that I remain safe, not try to prove that I can do everything under the sun.

It may sound like I'm saying independence isn't a good thing. It is, and I strongly advocate for it. But how independent would I be if I'd fallen and gotten hurt or chosen to attempt cooking and failed. Either could land me in the hospital. Using frozen dinners is not a sign of failure. Choosing not to use the tools that are out there would be much more difficult. Also, by asking for the help I needed in a polite way, it opened doors that may not have been opened. I got to spend time talking to friends in new ways. I got to stretch myself and see just what I'm capable of. I got to try new things.

I'm really grateful this was such a positive experience. I'm glad I got to try this and see that I could, indeed, transfer the skills I learned at college this past year to our house. I'm glad I have parents who are willing to let me try. I'm glad I didn't clam up, but instead gave it a try. It ended up working better than I expected.

He Leads Me: Reflections on Trust and Faith

Today in Sunday school we started reading the book "Traveling Light". It's by Max Lucado and is based on the 23rd Psalm. One of the things I stumbled upon as a thought is how hard, but important it is, to trust. I don't exactly remember what was said, but there were some observations that touched me and are now prompting me to write this down.

One of the questions was which part of the Psalm speaks to us the most. That was hard to do, but I picked one: "He leads me beside the still waters", specifically the "He leads me". As a guide dog handler and person who is blind, I do a lot of following and being lead. One of the most important aspects of a guide dog team is the trust. If I don't trust Julio, both of us are off rhythm. He can't lead me as well because I'm not letting him truly lead me. For example, he can try to lead me around something harmful (like a pole that could give me a goose egg), but if I'm second-guessing him, he can't always get me around that pole. In that case, it's not his fault that I'm not listening and if I get hurt. It's the same way with faith. If I don't trust God, or follow what He wants for my life, things will happen that He doesn't want to happen. He can warn me, but I have to trust Him.

It's the same way with bad things that happen. My foot pain and RSD is not necessarily something that my not listening to Him or not trusting Him caused, but when I try to prove that I can handle it on my own, or am unwilling to trust Him with the pain, anger, sadness and fear, things get off rhythm. I cause myself unnecessary pain.

But, when I trust Julio, and we're on, he can get me through even the worst and most crowded situation like a shopping mall full of people. And you know what? When I'm focusing on him and following him, I don't get frustrated by the obstacles as much. It's a wonderful feeling. I lean my head back a bit, straighten my shoulders, and swing my arm and smile. It's a great way to walk.

And, if I trust God, He won't always remove me from the painful or difficult situation, but He will guide me. Focusing on Him, I can put the hard stuff into perspective.

It's important, then, to know the character of my guide. I have to believe Julio's in the mood to guide well and that he wants to work and focus on the job before I can trust him. If I think he's distracted, it's hard to trust him and I need to take the initiative in the relationship and make him focus. But with God, I have to learn to trust Him. I have to believe that he loves me and always wants what's best for me. Knowing God's character and internalizing that is something I am still working on to be honest.

Smile! You're on Crossing Camera!

Wow! And to think that yesterday was supposed to be my quiet, relaxing, regroup and deal with the pain productively day. I went to Brewberry's as usual, and at around 10 got a call from a friend and fellow-board-member of a guide dog user's organization that a station she'd contacted about the issue of hybrid vehicles and the danger they pose for blind pedestrians wanted to do a story. Throughout the morning, she made contacts and kept me updated. Things developed that I needed to be downtown by 3. I found a bus route that would get me there around 2:30.

I must have changed clothes about 5 million times, trying to find the outfit that made me look good, looked normal for a student to wear and would work well on camera. I kept having fears that several bad clothing issues would happen, such as a real wardrobe malfunction. I also have this huge fear of having colorful undergarments show through, or ending up giving a whole new meaning to the concept of "news FLASH".

Bad pun, I know... Anyway, I was all nervous, and trying to look halfway decent. I finally stopped fussing and walked down near Brewberry's to catch the bus. This is where the frustration begins.

I don't know if the bus passed us, if I missed it (highly unlikely since I was 10 minutes early according to my clock), or if the bus was really late. So I missed my connecting bus. This meant I stood for about 45 minutes before the interview even started.

The bus I took downtown to the Nicollet Mall was interesting. The bus driver was very nice when I got on and we conversed a lot. He commented about Julio saying "your boyfriend needs a shave." It was a good laugh. When we got to the transit center that I got frighteningly lost at last year, a few people got on. One tried to take a cigarette on the bus, and the person sitting next to me smelled like he took a shower in alcohol. I am incredibly sensitive to that smell, and the driver seemed nervous. On the one hand, I don't want to judge, but on the other, I have to admit I was nervous. People were trying to bother Julio, but other passengers were watching out for me. I realize that my fears of that area are something I will need to deal with as a social work major.

I got off the bus, and got turned around. I needed to be at 11th street, and ended up at 7th. Crossing downtown is challenging for me. Note to self: NO Matter HOW LATE YOU ARE, DON'T RUN DOWN FOUR BLOCKS!

The interview went well. I was pretty nervous, but appreciated the reporter and photographer's time and their kindness. I haven't done a lot of camera work for a while, though there is the infamous "Beanie Baby" tape from seventh grade. That previous camera work does, however, make me critical of myself. I haven't seen the news clip (I don't have access to a TV), so it's hard to comment. That said, it does make me nervous crossing streets on camera and trying to tell my story in sound clips. I am always nervous that stories will turn into an inspirational disability piece and take the focus off the issues we're discussing. I was as careful to keep the focus on the story and issues and less on me, but I'm not sure how that worked.

After the story, we went to a place (I think it's a bar?), and I had a Cherry Coke. My fellow board-member and I talked for a while about lots of things. I appreciated her encouragement, and have some new ideas about what I want to do about my interest in chronic pain and blindness. This interest, honestly, is why I'm even staying in the honors program. I want to work on a project to explore the implications of dealing with a disability and chronic pain. It was very helpful to debrief and rest, since my pain levels were getting high.

I took a cab home, since it was after dark, I'd had to take a Percocet and I was sore and tired. The driver was very nice and even turned off the meter when we got to the campus since he was unsure of where my dorm is. It felt good to go home.

I took several things away from yesterday. First, although I was stressed, I worked through the issues getting to the TV station relatively well. I did not fold up and cry, but instead just kept pushing through the pain, fatigue and frustration. It ended up working out fine. It is a testament to the prayers, support and lessons from last summer that I was able to bounce back quickly enough to be on camera.

It is so nice to have "I can't" float away into "I'll try my best". More importantly, I'm learning that my best is all I can do, and that my best may end up being good enough.

The experience also made me think of last week's post about hope and fear in advocacy. With stories like this, there is the hope that people will learn something new and that this story will contribute to change. There is also the fear of doing something wrong, or not having the point come across. I also experienced hope and fear just getting to the interview and back.

Finally, it is nice to be reminded that I am capable of putting these things together. I put together praying, planning a route, problem-solving, asking for assistance, determining my spoons or energy level, using relaxation/imagery and debriefing/decompressing skills to make yesterday work. I still have a lot to learn, but I'm doing my best and learning in the process.

Accessible social media: It's not just for fun anymore.

Today, in two of my classes, we ended up using videos found on youtube. While I can't speak to the legality of the clips of at least one of them being there, I can say that there were good reasons for using them in the classroom. And it drove home a point, which I already knew, that accessibility of these new medias is going to be vital for things other than recreation.

I want to say up front that I think recreation is a perfectly valid reason to have accessibility. I believe that people with disabilities need access to everything and we deserve just as much of life as the next person.

But more than ever, I'm seeing that it's going to be vital to not have things preventing us from accessing media. One of the videos, for example, was completely printed information on AIDS in Africa. The result was probably stunning, but it meant that one of the presenters in our class had to read the text not only for me, but anyone else who had trouble reading the text. Obviously, captioning is good and important, but the video would've been just as good, or better with an added narrator reading the script.

The other video was easier to follow, and I don't really know if I missed anything. But by the same token, I've watched movies, thought I missed nothing and realized that there was so much more to the visual presentation once I heard it described. And if I wanted to use that for a paper, I would be out of luck, as it stands.

Another area where access to social media is going to be important is in crisis planning. I read Virginia Tech: Social Media in Crisis Planning on blogher, and thought "This could actually be great for students with visual impairments if it was used properly." Okay, I probably wasn't that eloquent when I was thinking that, but whatever. The thing is, if a R.A. writes something on a whiteboard and isn't able to inform me, I may miss vital information.

Right now, if there is some kind of danger, people try to inform me. One of the women from the disability services office on campus emails me if she knows that there will be construction or something. But if she isn't informed, the link breaks down. And if she isn't there, it also breaks down. If, say, text messaging were set up in a mass-message scenario where campus security could send us all text messages at once, or some other media, that might solve some of the problem. But then, that assumes that everyone has a text messaging system they can use, which we can't guarantee.

Can Facebook, Twitter and other sites help fill some of the void? That depends on a lot of factors. But that's why it's vital services be accessible. Right now, I'm only able to access campus email through a forwarding system that sends the email to my personal account, because our school's web mail is inaccessible. I won't even go into how much that frustrates me, because that would be a novel or three. The point is, though, that sets up one more link in the chain that can be broken.

Twitter and other services still have captchas that are inaccessible to people with visual impairments. Not everyone has the option of asking a friend or family member or colleague to help them sign up, and that is an insulting option, in my opinion.

And it's not like there isn't information out there, either. It's kind of like saying "People can come here in wheelchairs, as long as they have friends to carry them up the stairs."

I think social media like youtube, Del.icio.us, Twitter and other services have a really cool chance to be more ways for us to express ourselves, make friends, get information and live our lives. Like all options, there are positives and negatives to new technologies. But it will always be important that we get to have access to the new stuff.

I'm tired, and probably should've waited to write about this until I was thinking from the perspective of being more awake, but these are initial thoughts.

Shining light on hope: What Barabbas can teach us.

As part of my Bible in/as literature course this semester, I had the opportunity to read the novel Barabbas which is written by Paar Lagerkvist. It's a fictional account of the events of and following the crucifixion of Jesus from the perspective of Barabbas, the criminal who was spared death when the crowd requested he be freed instead of Jesus. [It's a fascinating read, which had me thinking "What if..." a lot as I read it.]

One of the most fascinating aspects of this novel was the way the author used visual imagery to supplement the action of the novel. Specifically, Lagerkvist used light, and the way the characters viewed that light, to demonstrate their perception of the Truth of Christ. Barabbas' reaction to Christ was quite mixed to say the least. He feared Christ, and wondered why he'd been spared. So, as one might imagine, his reaction to the light was also mixed. Light was something painful to Barabbas, and he seemed to prefer the darkness. I don't want to give away spoilers, but Barabbas' reaction to the light was one of fear and distrust, while others who found Christ seemed to welcome the light.

These reactions are very similar to how many of us view hope. Whether we profess Christianity or another faith or none at all, we have the choice to hope or not. Hope can be scary, like light. When I wonder what I should be hopeful for, it can be scary to realize that I may not be able to hope for the storybook ending to my dilemmas.

Being faced with living life with pain and the frustrations of dealing with that pain isn't fun. It's much easier to live in the darkness of denial. That darkness can be helpful, in the sense that darkness allows us to face that which is immediate. Sometimes, we need to walk through the dark nights so we can learn more a bout ourselves without the distractions of viewing our circumstances. The darkness can be a time to contemplate our reactions and resources, without being distracted by the details of our day to day existence. Ask anyone who wakes up in the middle of the night, and you'll probably hear that these hours spent in the darkness are ideal for learning about the self or the soul.

But the light of hope demands truth about our circumstances. When we truly hope, we acknowledge the things we don't like, but actively seek good things that will make something better. When I "came into the light" and admitted that the pain wasn't getting better, for example, it was incredibly painful, as it is for those with sight when bright lights come on after pitch darkness. But out of that pain came the realization that I could live a good life, even despite the pain. I began to see that I had choices. I could stay upset, continue to deny that things weren't getting better or I could learn relaxation and pain management techniques and learn to adapt to life in pain.

That "coming into the light" happened in late September. The road has been very bumpy. I've had to continue to face the darkness and shadows of living with pain, but have also experienced the hope of realizing that I really could make it through a challenging semester. The lights of hope and truth continue to illuminate my circumstances. I continue to acknowledge the challenges, but I am also able to hope for continued progress and continued chances to grow from the pain.

As our class continued to read literature, my work with the novel Barabbas continued to be helpful in the class. We began to see more references to light in

Christian traditions such as Easter (the lengthening of days and growth of nature) and Christmas (the beginning of earth's tilting toward the sun). But we also saw it in the scriptures (the acknowledgement of sin, negativity, pain and sadness giving way to the birth of Christ and promises of peace as well as the death of Christ giving way to the Resurrection).

No matter how you choose to seek the light of hope, I pray that we will all allow hope to acknowledge the bad, and actively seek out the good in our lives and the lives of those around us.

Peace and Hope

Today's news is filled with acts of violence, threats, anger and death. A plane was hijacked, five young Amish women were killed, North Korea is testing nuclear missiles, and everyone is getting angry at everyone else. It's hard to find a strand of peace or hope in the news.

It would be so easy to give in to hopelessness, anger, fear and violence. In each of our personal lives, there are little broken places, things that keep gnawing at us. It would be so easy to give into those same emotions. But I don't think it's the right answer.

It would also be easy to say that "these emotions aren't admirable", or something like that. But the truth is, we each have those emotions, and we can, and should, use them for good. Anger spurs on courage, fear tells us something is wrong, pain does the same thing (sometimes). Each of these things are okay to feel.

I realized something in theology yesterday. We were reading about the Resurrection. In the book of

Mark, chapter 16, if you look at the footnotes, you'll probably notice something interesting.

Notice that there are about 11 verses that the footnotes say weren't included in the most reliable manuscripts. I find that very interesting. Notice what it ends with if you take out those eleven verses "Trembling and bewildered, the women went out and fled from the tomb. They said nothing to anyone, because they were afraid."

They were afraid? What kind of ending is that for "The greatest story ever told?" It wasn't what I expected. Now, to be fair, we talked about possible reasons for that. The one that seems most plausible to me is that, since this book was written just around the time of the fall of Jerusalem, Mark was afraid too.

So, the act of covering up fear is not a new thing. As I read these news articles, I've decided to be honest about my reactions. If they scare me, that's okay, I'm scared. If I'm ticked off, that's fine. The question is, what will I do with the gifts of anger and fear? Will I lash out, like the man who stormed that school? Will I be afraid and stop living my life? I sure hope not, and I hope you won't either.

The gift of anger is courage. And the gift we gain from fear can be hope. Let's each challenge ourselves to take those gifts and go on. Listen to your reactions to things that happen. Instead of bottling them, or hiding from them, learn from them.

I'm looking back on my training with Julio. There was a lot of fear there. Do I wish I had not been afraid or nervous? Sometimes. But I also know that those feelings gave me gifts. The fear gave me a sense of how permanent this was. It kept me from getting cocky.

The more I thought about it yesterday, the more I think I like the ending of Mark the way it was the first time. The lack of a happy-ever-after story gave me a lot of questions. What happened next? What did they do? How did they resolve their fears? Sometimes, the disturbing stories show us the most about the human condition. They give us a context. Would the Passion and Resurrection stories have the same message without the fear? In the turmoil of the Passion, did the fear these women and men had keep them alive? Was the fear something God used to keep them safe?

I love how this theology class is showing me that in many ways, the "little miracles" are what are so amazing. What disturbing story are you watching for a happy-ever-after-ending? What if that story has more than the happy ending?

Election 2006: My own personal victory

I tried to avoid the political ads as much as possible this year. It seems like all that one can learn from them is the answer to that question, "How low can you go?" But I actually really did care about this election.

It's the first big election I've been able to vote in, since I wasn't able to vote in 2004. But this year, I got to vote. And it was the coolest experience.

For those who may not be aware, before this year, a blind person was not guaranteed a private, accessible ballot. There were three options in how to vote:

1. Apply for an absentee ballot and have someone help you fill it out.

2. Bring a friend to the polls and have them fill out your ballot.

3. Have two election judges fill out the ballot for you (the idea here is to make sure that this ensures that the ballot is marked properly.)

The problem with all three of these options is that the vote is no longer private. I have no choice but to tell someone else how I voted. I don't care how professional election judges are (I know several and do trust them), but I should have the same rights to access as the rest of the country. And, yes, I know about all of the debates about whether people actually do have access, but that's beyond my little brain right now.

Yesterday, I got to vote! And it was so cool! So, here's the story:

I chose to vote in my home-city, instead of at college. Part of this is because I wanted to vote on some issues that I could only vote on at home, and the other part is that I wanted to know how things went with the voting machine at home. I know that the whole state is using the automark machines for accessibility, but I wanted to see what it would be like voting at home. So my sister picked me up, and being the people we were, we grabbed lattes for the long drive home.

Traffic was horrendous! It seemed worse to me than usual, which may have been due to the elections, or my pain causing a shorter fuse than normal. It made the commute much better to have coffee with me though.

When we got there, there was quite a line. This was not a good thing, since pain levels were at least a 7.5, and that's an intentional underestimation. Dad had already voted, and asked the election judge if I could use the machine and avoid all standing for so long. To be clear, no one was using it at the time. I got in quickly, which was good.

The election judge was a bit unsure about guiding Julio and I, but once I showed her sighted guide, everything was fine. She took me to the table where you sign that you've registered, and get a voters receipt. The cool thing was that they even had a signature guide and knew how to use it. A signature guide is a little window (usually plastic), that you can put on the line where you need to sign to have a guide of where the line is and how much room you have.

The judge showed me how to work the machine, which was simple. It has a large-buttoned tactile keypad which is pretty easy to use. Every key beeps when pressed, and there is speech feedback to read the ballot and tell you what you've chosen. I turned off the screen and went through the ballot. After I got done after about 20 minutes (I didn't know there was so much stuff on a ballot!), put my ballot in the machine and got my "I voted" sticker.

A friend, who reads this journal, got to see me grinning like a fool. I was so excited that I got to vote privately, accessibly and independently. I got to see a summary screen before my ballot was printed, which made it easy to make sure I'd done things correctly.

I know that I had almost nothing to do with accessible voting being a reality. I didn't know anything about advocacy when the Help America Vote act got passed. All I've done is tell people about the issues of voting as a blind person, and write one letter to the editor. I am so grateful to those who have fought to make the great experience I had a reality.

So... What's my Tapestry?

I just read an amazing article in my "The Reflective Woman" book. I'll admit, this class made me nervous at first because I was afraid it'd just be a bunch of women writing and talking about how men all suck because they're oppressing us and how we need to push ahead and do better at beating them or at least being equals. But this article--Weaving an Identity Tapestry--is not even close to that. It's written by Sonja D. Curry-Johnson who is a feminist, African American and Christian. She wrote a wonderful piece that talks about how sometimes our different parts of our identities seem to conflict. She talked about how she sometimes struggles with a faith that enslaved her ancestors, her desire to care for her children but not wanting to be pushed into it, her frustration with a faith that wants to put women in the backseat. I've shared similar frustrations.

I'm not African American, but I am blind. I've had to fight several internal battles and external battles relating to this. Everyday, I have to fight the battle to decide how to be most independent. I always used to think that independence was doing everything for myself. But by the same token, some things are hard. Do I ask for help? If I do, I fear being ridiculed by some blind people. I fear being told that I'm a disgrace to other blind community members. But if I avoid asking for help, I can mess up even worse and be an even bigger disgrace. I have to daily fight that battle with myself.

I have to fight the battle of societal expectations. For the longest time, I hated even thinking about going into work in the blindness field because I knew people would think I could only do that since I can't see. It's probably similar to the experiences many blind musicians have. You know, the questions "What are you planning for your career?"

"I'd like to be a rehabilitation teacher."

"Oh, that's so nice. Yes, that's something you'll be good at." There are so many misconceptions, I always felt I had to fight the battle and do something different so that I could help tear those misconceptions down. But I really want to be a rehabilitation teacher or counselor. I want to at least help out in the blind community. Yes, my blindness has influenced my opinion, but not in the way people assume. I just know that I probably wouldn't have known about or cared about these issues if I was not blind.

One of the areas I feel stretched is my faith. In a community of Christians, I can either be respected as a blind person or have people assume I'm wrong/an evil person/need to be healed. Many people automatically assume that if I had faith enough, God would heal me. I don't understand that very well. I believe God is choosing to let me be blind for a reason. As hard as it is to accept, He has a reason for my foot pain, too. I don't understand it. But I also have to be careful that I'm not so militant about this point that I won't accept prayers or allow for an opening should God choose to miraculously heal me. It's a fine line to walk and I'm not sure I walk it as well as I could.

An area where the author felt stretched by her faith was the area of feminism. It was actually mentioned in a previous article, too. How can we stay in a faith where women are oppressed? In some denominations, we're not allowed to be pastors. How can we reconcile that? What she concludes and I'd have to agree is that things will change. Someday, we'll go back to what God intended, and we won't be oppressed. But we can't just disown the faith until then. That's hard to put into words so it sounds right. But basically, it's like we're changing things from the inside. Again, a fine line to walk.

And finally, not being limited by feminism or the corrupted way it's become too militant. Feminism isn't always about burning bras or being unwilling to accept help from a man. But believing in ourselves is important, equality is important.

I guess what I'm taking away is that when we have things in us that can be considered weaknesses by others, we can't let them be weaknesses, we need to embrace them. If there are problems in how we're viewed, we can change things from the inside. That's what we're getting at. I'm going to try hard to embrace all of the pieces of my tapestry.

Nickie's Nook

www.ingramcontent.com/pod-product-compliance
Lightning Source LLC
Chambersburg PA
CBHW032112090426
42743CB00007B/321